DOREEN KERRY

Heart in Lockdown

White Lace and Promises

Mereo Books

2nd Floor, 6-8 Dyer Street, Cirencester, Gloucestershire, GL7 2PF
An imprint of Memoirs Books. www.mereobooks.com
and www.memoirsbooks.co.uk

Title of Book: HEART IN LOCKDOWN
ISBN: 978-1-86151-742-5

First published in Great Britain in 2020
by Mereo Books, an imprint of Memoirs Books.

Copyright ©2020

Doreen Kerry has asserted her right under the Copyright Designs and Patents Act 1988 to be identified as the author of this work.

A CIP catalogue record for this book is available from the British Library. This book is sold subject to the condition that it shall not by way of trade or otherwise be lent, resold, hired out or otherwise circulated without the publisher's prior consent in any form of binding or cover, other than that in which it is published and without a similar condition, including this condition being imposed on the subsequent purchaser.

The address for Memoirs Books can be
found at www.mereobooks.com

Mereo Books Ltd. Reg. No. 12157152

Typeset in 11/15pt Century Schoolbook
by Wiltshire Associates.
Printed and bound in Great Britain

Other books by Doreen Kerry:

Pathway to the Moon (2018)
When Angels Fall (2018)
Dinner in the Sky (2018)
Random Keys (2019)
A Pocketful of Rainbows (2019)
Pennies from Heaven (2020)

CONTENTS

	Dedication
	Preface
Chapter 1:	Same difference 1
Chapter 2:	Bumps in the road 7
Chapter 3:	Weird science 14
Chapter 4:	Five Go into Lockdown 16
Chapter 5:	Brownie's honour 21
Chapter 6:	In Old London Town 24
Chapter 7:	Tales from the Underground 33
Chapter 8:	Air (on the side of caution) 45
Chapter 9:	A test in time 49
Chapter 10:	The oysters went A.W.O.L 56
Chapter 11:	Piggin' awful 60
Chapter 12:	What can't be fixed 65
Chapter 13:	Melancholy baby 68
Chapter 14:	Staying positive 76
Chapter 15:	Shuttlecocks galore 98
Chapter 16:	Where's Mother? 108
Chapter 17:	Blenheim 125
Chapter 18:	The sewing box 131
Chapter 19:	Curry and lentils 139
Chapter 20:	Clueless 142
Chapter 21:	Carriage return 146
Chapter 22	The birthday boy 149
Chapter 23:	Nightmare on Downing Street 151
Chapter 24:	The Nightingale Restaurant 158
Chapter 25:	Keeping track 163
Chapter 26:	Beam me up Snotty 166
Chapter 27:	In loving memory 171

DEDICATION

'My first, my last, my everything.'

Once more I dedicate this book to my husband, in eternal gratitude that he had chosen to spend the rest of his life with me, even if it was cut short through no fault of his own.

In some ways I am thankful that he has not been around to witness the fall-out of this awful pandemic. Although I have needed him more than ever I know he couldn't be in a safer place at the moment.

Losing him once has been hard enough and if he is watching down on me right now I have only this to say to him:

'You'll be in heaven for our wedding anniversary
So, what shall I do?
If I could fly through the clouds
I would spend it with you
But save me a seat,
A soft comfy chair
'Cos although you may not see me
Rest assured, somehow, I shall be there.'

Doreen Kerry
7th November 2020

PREFACE

I feel blessed that being creative comes easily to me, and despite the notion that memoir writing should focus on a particular theme, once I get going, I write about anything and everything. It may not seem my themes are in any way connected at first, but they always end up being the thread that holds everything together.

At first glance the opening chapter may sound a little odd, but it is a very necessary way to help my readers re-connect with the central character in all my books – my husband. I never expected that my imagination would have run away with me quite so much during these unprecedented times upon which I was inspired to create another fictional drama out of yet another crisis.

Forty-three years ago I stood at the altar in white lace, full of promises to love, honour and obey the only man to steal my heart; a heart which, as a result of tragic circumstances, has been in complete and utter lockdown ever since.

Eventually the restrictions that have been imposed on the nation during life in the time of Covid-19 will be lifted and for most a sense of normality will resume, but for me the light at the end of the tunnel still seems a long way off, and only when justice has been served can the process of recovery truly begin.

CHAPTER 1

SAME DIFFERENCE

One day Waggie and Wollie decided to go for a walk to Bumble-Bee Common. Their pal Wiggie said he would catch them up as soon as he had finished what he was doing back at the cottage where they lived.

No sooner had the pair left home than Eddie the Teddy, who lived in the same village, raced by so fast on his scooter when trying to overtake his parents who were walking some way ahead that he inadvertently bumped into Wollie, knocking him off his feet. Wollie was left lying on his back in the middle of the road while Eddie sped off, completely oblivious to what he had done.

Wollie complained of knee and shoulder pain, and he also had a nasty bump on his head. Waggie told him not to move but to lie still and stay where he was whilst he went to fetch the local doctor.

In the meantime, Wiggie, having finished what he was doing at the cottage, headed off to catch up with his companions. However, along the way he tripped on a pothole, sending the playing cards that he had in his hand up into the air. They ended up scattered across the road.

No sooner had Wiggie knelt down to pick them up than Dr Longface drove slowly past in his car. Having been on the lookout for an injured Wolligog, and, seeing Wiggie on his knees, the doctor wasted no time in stopping. He got out of his car and proceeded to bandage Wiggie's head, even though there was no obvious sign of a bump. He assumed that it must be hidden somewhere amidst his patient's mass of black hair.

After that the doc tied a further bandage around one of Wiggie's knees, done up so tight that he could hardly walk. Then he rubbed Wiggie's shoulder awfully hard, despite him saying that there was nothing wrong with it.

Wiggie was certainly not happy at being bundled into the doctor's car and being driven home.

Now confronted with not one but three Wolligogs — Wiggie's housemates having already returned to the cottage by this time — Dr Longface gave no consideration to the fact that he had attended to the wrong 'person'. He considered it was not his fault, as they 'all looked the same.'

As soon as the doctor left, Waggie took the bandages off Wiggie and put them on Wollie before helping him into bed and giving him a hot water bottle and a mug of hot milk.

After a good night's sleep Wollie woke up refreshed and ready to face another day.

Adapted from 'The Three Golliwogs', Chapter 4 'A Muddle of Golliwogs', Enid Blyton 1968

I have made it no secret in the past that Enid Blyton was my favourite author as I was growing up. I was too young back then to appreciate how gender and social and racial stereotypes were behind many of the characters she created. How she was allowed to get away with it for so long is beyond me.

Just as Enid had wrongly pigeon-holed all Wolligogs as rude, mischievous and villainous, characterising them with large white-rimmed eyes that stood out against their very dark skin and with wild fizzy hair and red clown-like lips to liken them to black people, the booking clerk who admitted my hubby onto the Acute Assessment Unit of the Firchester hospital in 2012 wrongly pigeon-holed my man as someone who was there for a drinking and smoking related problem as opposed to a serious life-threatening illness. Evidently the clerk was not able to grasp the word 'acute', else his focus should have been on transcribing information relative only to the episode of illness that was present on admission. Thanks to other information that had become available, not only was Ted's condition blown out of all context, but so was the diagnosis that followed.

Barely able to stand, increasingly short of breath, and remarkably slim for his age, my man may have *given* the appearance that he was drunk, but this could not have been further from the truth.

It wouldn't have surprised me if the middle-aged administrator had watched too many Charlie Chaplin and Laurel and Hardy films in his time, with their comic portrayals of drunkenness that ranged from staggering and wobbly walks to performing nimble and precarious feats that they could not possibly have done whilst sober.

Ted had not stood at the reception of the Firchester Hospital that day dressed in a tutu prancing around with balletic grace nor tootling a lamp as if it were a trumpet, and whilst I under any other circumstances would have paid dearly to have seen it, on this occasion his rickety and giddy state was down to the fact that he had seriously low blood pressure and was likely dehydrated, the problem for which he was sent there by his GP in the first place.

It really was no laughing matter that the clinicians did not go with their initial diagnosis but put two and two together and came up with completely the wrong number.

It never ceases to amaze me the lengths that staff at the Firchester Hospital went to, and continue to go to today, to shift the blame for their mistakes onto anyone but themselves. They considered his death six days later to have been just an 'unfortunate event' in the same way Dr Longface thought of the incident with Wiggie.

My hubby was the victim and the medical staff were the culprits – the ones who should have stuck with their diagnosis of sepsis as documented in his notes and confirmed through blood tests, instead of then changing their minds and depriving him of the chance to receive the right antibiotic at the right time within the crucial time-frame.

Contrary to Enid's notion that everything in life was black and white, I can 100% vouch for the fact that it is not, and if only the clinicians who were responsible for hubby's care had sought to think outside of the 'box', his chance of survival would have been greater.

Over time I started to wonder what kind of situation would have to come along to persuade the doctors and nurses to think differently – something that could shake them up and put their skills and knowledge to the test so they would soon realise that courses of treatment should be tailor-made for the unique needs of the patient regardless of whether the symptoms they might present with mimicked those of others they had nursed before.

Perhaps a global pandemic was what they needed.

Having teased my readers with partial answers as to what went wrong up to now, whilst I cannot predict the ending of this book any more than I could all the others, it does not stop me from wanting to get to the bottom of things as those responsible persist in hiding behind their white collars and coats.

Oops! There I go again. I feel a song coming on! Just when I am trying to end my introduction on a serious note, 'White Tie and Tails' springs to mind. I shall spare you the agony of hearing me sing, sing, sing like a Womble and whether or not I write, write, write like a Womble is a question I urge you to think very carefully about before telling me that my tale to date has been little more than a load of old rubbish. I can't say I have ever had a thing about Fred Astaire, and Ginger Rogers will always be Ginger Rogers to me, not Madame Cholet.

Whilst everyone does tell me that I'm 'good for my age', and I may be a bit rounder than I would like, I do not have a dressing room, let alone one with a star on the door, but I hope my continued tap, tap, tapping on my keyboard as I harp on about my unexpected loss will be hard to ignore.

My story may not reach a Hollywood set or a Broadway stage as I let my imagination take me away, but I certainly hope it will entertain in some small way or other.

(*Wombling White Tie and Tails*, 1975)

CHAPTER 2

BUMPS IN THE ROAD

Having had to sit through no end of news bulletins on the telly over the past few years wondering whether or not the Prime Minister would ever get us out of the EU, I breathed a sigh of relief as he stood in front of No.10 on the evening of 31st January 2020 and declared 'Tonight we are leaving the European Union'. 'For many people this is an astonishing moment of hope, a moment they thought would never come' he said in wrapping up his speech, and 'Whatever the bumps in the road ahead, we will begin to unite and level up.'

I am in no way politically minded – the last time I voted in a general election, Harold Wilson was in power – but I was just fed up with all the 'should we or shouldn't we' arguments dominating the news.

I remember the time when the first referendum in

British history was held on the issue of whether we should remain in the Common Market or not. That was in 1975 and they called it the EEC back then, which stood for European Economic Community. The question of leaving or staying took nothing short of fourteen years to debate, so in some ways I guess we should be grateful this latest issue not been allowed to drag on for quite so long.

I doubt the leader of the Conservative Party could ever have envisaged that three months after that he would be standing in front of the famous black door again – on the 16th March 2020 to be precise – to discuss the nations' efforts to fight back against an infectious disease called Covid-19. It was thought to have originated in China a few weeks previously, with thousands of people in other countries already having died from it, but at that stage the World Health Organisation had not felt the need to declare it as a public health emergency of international concern.

Since it has swept the UK, neither I nor the rest of the people of the British Isles can shy away from what is going on right under our noses.

What can I say about the Coronavirus at present as I sit poised at my laptop this morning ready to take my story forward in a new light?

Not a lot really. I know the term derives from the word 'corona' (referring to the shape of the virus under a magnifying glass) and the year when it was believed to have first hit China.

Rumour has it that it evolved from a zoonotic disease that jumped between live and dead animals placed side by side on wet market stalls in Wuhan and somehow then found its way into the human body.

It all sounds quite bizarre, I know, but I am just saying what is being 'speculated' right now. What I do know for sure is that Coronavirus mirrors the symptoms of flu where, similarly, people experience a cough, a high temperature (38c or above) and shortness of breath, and that it can affect people in different ways depending upon the severity of their symptoms in relation to any underlying health needs that in turn will affect how their bodies will respond to the invading virus.

I guess I am no different to a lot of people when it comes to watching the news ordinarily – generally dismissing topics of conversation that do not relate directly to what is going on in my own country – but now I can no longer seek to bury my head in the sand, as this latest bug to hit the high streets is seriously going to affect my life and that of my family in the weeks to come.

Unusually this evening I listened attentively as our Prime Minister set out the Government's objective to try and tackle the disease, calling it 'the worst public health crisis for a generation' whilst standing behind his podium on Downing Street.

'By bringing forward the right measures at the right time' he said, 'the peak of the epidemic could be delayed and flattened.'

He went on to say that 'with hope, suffering could be minimised and lives could be saved', emphasising that all steps the Government were about to put into place would be 'based scrupulously on the best scientific evidence' as those in the 'business' had started working frantically to find a vaccine, since no medicine had yet demonstrated efficiency at treating the virus.

To diversify for a moment, in 2017 the BBC News reported that sepsis was responsible for 44,000 deaths each year in the UK *alone* – so serious that the NICE guidelines (National Institute for Clinical Excellence) were suggesting that doctors should have been treating it with the same urgency as if someone was suspected of having a heart attack.

Shortness of breath and a temperature of 38 degrees or above are just two out of four symptoms any qualified doctor should recognise in his/her diagnosis of sepsis – an equally serious health condition which the World Health Organisation had also declared all those years ago as a 'global epidemic', estimated to affect more than 30 million people worldwide each year and to have the potential at that particular time to result in 6 million deaths. Everything hinged on the person's condition being managed correctly by medical staff.

Contrary to the coronavirus, aggressive treatment for sepsis *was* available at the point of my husband's admission to hospital. As I said, if given early enough, it could have saved him.

I ask no forgiveness therefore for continuingly questioning the qualifications of the attending doctor who felt giving my hubby a broad-spectrum antibiotic as the 'usual line of treatment' was acceptable, as the result of a blood test was pending.

I have to wonder then if some of those forty thousand people who had reportedly died from sepsis (statistically) five years after he had, had done so because of systemic failures such as happened in Ted's case, where inappropriate treatment had led them to become victims of a respiratory arrest induced by septic shock that then led to multi-organ failure in the same way.

I further wonder whether the hospital staff at the NHS Trust hospitals that those people had attended equally had the audacity to wrongly link their deaths to their social habits, as happened in hubby's case.

In one breath the public are led to believe that every post mortem examination is approached with an 'open' mind, yet by the same token the 'system' also states that the initial approach to such an examination relies heavily on information provided by the clinicians to the pathologist beforehand.

So, what if my nearest and dearest had maintained a healthy relationship with alcohol over the years – something that he never denied, nor I seek to do in his defence? And so what if he had preferred to smoke instead of eating his own bodyweight in cream cakes to combat occupational stress – somehow considered a 'likely contributor' to his demise? His lifestyle choice was met less favourably than someone who may have been grossly obese yet was entitled to expensive surgery to 'make them better' without question.

Just as Dr Longface chose not to consider Wiggie, Wollie and Waggie in an individual light – thus giving the wrong treatment to the wrong Wolligog – I did not consider it rocket science that the supposedly highly-trained clinicians who were responsible for Ted's care could not have distinguished between someone with a basic chest infection and sepsis-associated pneumonia.

Now the way I see it, the symptoms of sepsis and the coronavirus are not a million miles apart, the first having been described as a 'hidden killer' and this latest one as a 'silent killer', yet evidently the two viruses are *not* the same in other respects, else doctors would be using the same treatment for sepsis on Covid-19 patients right now, which is not the case.

As this latest disease continues to dominate the headlines, why is it that suddenly Covid-19 sends a reminder to NHS staff to consider the importance of identifying the manifestations of potentially life-threatening illnesses (such as this) in order that maximum support and care and a rapid referral to the critical care or intensive care unit can be optimised, yet when faced with someone with sepsis they can be more selective as to how they want to play things?

My husband was not a carrier of the coronavirus, which was long after his time anyway – he would have brought no harm to anyone – and it was not necessary during the course of his treatment that staff should have donned a long-sleeved water-resistant gown and goggles, or wear a fluid-repellent mask or respirator.

Sepsis was not contagious, yet the right antibiotics for Ted were kept at arm's length. Why? That is the burning question.

I have always thought that writing a story is a bit like building a house, and I hope my series to date has provided a solid foundation for others to learn about inequalities in justice as I seek to make a change for the better. I feel confident that the bricks and mortar have been properly laid, else my construction thus far would not have got the approval of my architectural editor.

I am taking a huge risk by including this latest crisis in my storyline with no idea what it might amount to by the end, but inviting you through the doorway to my past before the place is even finished provides me with the glossy distraction I need right now to be able to think about how I shall tackle 'life in the time of corona.'

Not dissimilar to author Gabriel Garcia Marquez's *Love in the time of Cholera* (1985), I like to consider mine to a be a sentimental story about the enduring power of true love, and I shall continue to fight his corner for as long as I have air in my lungs.

CHAPTER 3

WEIRD SCIENCE

As I write this on 27th March 2020, despite all their speeches about people keeping a safe distance from others and not going out unless absolutely necessary as announced in a plan by the PM 11 days ago, neither he, the heir to the throne nor, ironically, the current Health and Social Care Secretary, have been exempt from testing positive to the virus; nor the Chief Medical Officer for that matter, who also showed symptoms of Covid-19 after being seen coughing into his hands on national television whilst giving a speech on handwashing!

But that's the thing about Covid, you see – it can sneak up on a person when they least expect it and it is difficult to be able to pinpoint exactly where or when they may have come into contact with someone responsible for passing it on.

The PM's key adviser, having chaired several meetings in previous days, was recently observed in the media running as fast towards the 'back exit' of Downing Street as if he had a rocket up him. Sporting a huge laptop bag over his shoulder and a less than sporting bomber jacket, he had reportedly developed mild symptoms of the dreaded virus and undoubtedly just wanted to get home, fearful of how it might impact on his loved ones.

He is, after all, just a man underneath the fancy title, but as I watched the footage on TV all I could think of was the message that mum had instilled in us kids, which was to 'always walk and never run in case you trip over.'

Laptops do cost a pretty penny, but I guess the cost of a replacement computer in the unfortunate event that he had gone a*s over t*t, would have been the last thing on his mind.

Are we now about to see more of the London-based politicians fleeing from the 'scene' just as the rats had done during the time of the Black Death with a death toll that has to be pretty hard to beat?

We shall see.

CHAPTER 4

FIVE GO INTO LOCKDOWN

Since my last account, the leader of our country has hopped next door into No. 11, where he is taking up temporary residence in order to isolate himself from his partner who is 'with child' – his child in fact – since he too is now showing symptoms of the virus.

As a 'preggie-maybe-one-day-weddie', his good lady is now twice as vulnerable. Who might be responsible for this, I wonder? Mr J having caught the virus I mean – not the pregnancy!

Well, I am allowed, am I not, to put things in my own matter-of-fact way without causing offence?

Talk about 'Power's Elbow' – a title that is bestowed upon a Prime Minister's personal aid! Now unless Mr C had given his 'boss' the elbow (literally) before he sped off for home that day, I doubt he could be accused of having had anything to do with this latest event.

His Royal Highness – the Prince – and his other half are also in self-isolating as I speak since the heir to the throne has now developed symptoms. The couple are reportedly living 'separately' at their estate at Balmoral.

I have to say, I can think of worse places to get laid up than at a beautiful stately home as the Government slogan:

STAY ALERT - CONTROL THE VIRUS - SAVE LIVES

features everywhere across the UK, but given that they are both over 70, and already in what the PM describes as being in the 'shielding' group, symptoms or not they are not allowed to go out in any case for now.

On a positive note it now means that the quintessentially English 'quintet' will have more time to spend practising their 'palm-to-palm' hand-washing soap technique at home.

Hey, this has just provided me with inspiration for the title of this book (at present left blank): *'Five Go into Lockdown'*. It has a good ring to it, don't you think?

Maybe not, although I am sure there will be one out with that title soon along with the other Enid Blyton spoof books: *Five on Brexit Island, Five Give up the Booze* and *Five Lose Dad In the Garden Centre* – grown up versions of the author's previous works.

If it should be that this is not the case, then I assume all publishing rights, OK?

Apparently, Ms 'far- from- politically- correct' Blyton only intended to write between six and eight books in her series – not about hospital mishaps, but the amusing mishaps that the five children she wrote about had encountered during their school summer holiday. Instead, she ended up with far more books to her name, becoming a huge success and making a mint in royalties.

I myself only intended to write one book, but here I am seven books later and although none of my novels will ever be adapted for television or made into films to be shown across the world, as I said, I really cannot let this current crisis go to waste as I set to weave two things into one where the inspiration for my book could not have arisen from a more unlikely source. As for any royalties to date – well, I might have made enough to fill up my petrol tank.

Needless to say, the compulsory games that I, my family, and the rest of the country must play right now are in no way as exciting as those played out by Ms Blyton's characters Anne, George, Julian, Dick and Timmy the dog, but it is what it is.

Empathetic to all those who have lost their nearest and dearest to Covid-19 so far, I shall take off my grieving widow's hat for a short while and change it for something less 'angry', like the Sorting Hat lent to me by my friend Harry before he and the rest of the house of Gryffindor went into lockdown too, as not even wizards are exempt from catching it.

I can't confess to having the same intelligence as the unique piece of headwear that has been loaned to me for the purpose of this exercise – reserved for those in the business of wizardry ordinarily – nor can I will words to come out of my forehead, but just like the hat I am rather old but only slightly battered. I am not a mind-reader, and I really wonder how the hat will respond to the thoughts that are going through my mind at this precise moment as I perch it upon my own thinking cap.

One thing we do have in common is that we are notorious for refusing to admit we have made a mistake – the hat when sorting out students into 'houses' and me for refusing to allow clinicians to tell me that it is I who had made the mistake of not dropping my complaint when they wanted me to.

It is a pity, my dear readers, that you too do not possess a Sorting Hat that will allow you to magically navigate through the many layers of this writer's mind. Instead you will have to interpret your findings some other way.

It's a shame I don't possess a talent in telekinesis either, as I wouldn't have to leave the house for shopping at all in future, being able to get the necessities I want to fly off the shelves and land at my doorstep before the supermarkets open up and all the greedy cake-makers snap up the last bags of flour from the shelves now that panic buying has set in, leaving me to eat my home-made curries without my equally home-made parathas.

That would be like Ant appearing on *Saturday Night Takeaway* without Dec, Stan shifting that piano without Ollie (Laurel and Hardy) or me picking up a pen without writing an epic!

Some things just are not meant to be.

So as I set off on another crazy road trip don't worry – I shall keep two metres away from you at all times in line with 'social distancing' and so, in my previous altered ego state as 'Dorothy' on that Yellow Brick Road I shall make sure I:

STAY HOME – PROTECT TOTO – SAVE AUNTIE EM

CHAPTER 5

BROWNIE'S HONOUR

As a young child growing up, the things I used to ask my mum included: What was it like to be back home with the family after having been evacuated in Cornwall for almost six years? How did it feel to pass the Eleven Plus exam afterwards? How was it that you got to become penfriends with actor Farley Granger? Did you really chase headless chickens around a farmyard as a kid? And what was it like to march behind King George's coffin at eight years old?

And of my dad: What made you run off and join the Merchant Navy at 16 years old? How did you feel when your sister Mona died of tuberculosis at the age of 5 in a hospital in Calcutta? Did you really live a few doors away from Cliff Richard's aunt in Lucknow? What was the best ship you ever sailed on? and Did your workmate on the council *really* have Kit-E-Kat in his sandwiches?

Sadly, my parents are no longer around, but whilst the rest of my family and I are currently living through these 'unprecedented times' as the Government calls it, thankfully our lives have not been affected too much so far. I hope it stays that way.

I guess the burning question my great-grandchildren will ask me in years to come, God willing I make it to the end of this book without having become a 'victim' of the disease myself, is: 'Hey Grand-Nanny, what was it like to be alive during the Coronavirus outbreak'?

As an ex-Brownie, I have continued to uphold the Brownie Guide Law, which is 'to think of others before myself and to do a good turn every day'.

I have always found it quite endearing when the wisdom and expertise that people have developed over the years gets shared with others, and now it is my turn to follow suit, working on the principle that at some point in time my distant offspring may need to write a 4000-word essay on Covid-19 as part of a history exam – hence the reason why some of the following chapters will be written in the past tense and hopefully not too difficult to follow.

I know different authors will have their own style of writing, but I am a firm believer that it often pays to go backwards before you can go forward, and I hope I have already provided a little insight into the direction that my story is about to go.

My account may sound boring to start with – and whilst I shall never be able to master the art of falling sideways through a gap left by a raised hatch at a south London pub, don't be fooled, things will start to get funnier. *('Only Fools and Horses; 'Yuppy Love' – 6th Series, 1989)*

So, stealing the catchphrase of the late comedian Max Bygraves (1922- 2012), it just leaves me to say: 'I wanna tell you a story.'

CHAPTER 6

IN OLD LONDON TOWN

At exactly one-thirty on Monday, Wednesday and Friday afternoons week after week back in the 1960s, my own nan and granddad would switch on their black and white rented television set and tune into a programme called 'Watch with Mother.' Snuggled up to my mum or sitting on my grandad's knee, 'Andy Pandy', 'The Woodentops' and 'The Flowerpot Men' (or 'Bill and Ben' as I use to call it) were the characters I enjoyed watching the most, as I have mentioned several times in the past. Those childhood programmes were a mixture of nursery rhymes, stories and music.

Why they had to change the title of the programme to 'See Saw' in 1980 I do not know, but my siblings and I needed no introduction to the new theme tune as it was exactly what mum and dad used to sing to us when pushing us up and down on a real seesaw as kids.

The song goes:

*'Seesaw Margery Daw,
Johnny shall have a new master,
He shall earn but a penny a day,
Because he can't work any faster'*

- just in case you are wondering.

Anyway, by the time I was 63, the one-thirty news on the telly covered a variety of things from serious to funny stories, some believable, some not, but what dominated it was talks of a pandemic which had evolved from an unknown virus named the Coronavirus.

So now it wasn't just mothers watching the lunchtime programme with their kids but anyone else who happened to be at home who would ordinarily have been at school or at work but for the events that were about to unfold.

So, to start my story off, the Prime Minister at the time of Covid-19 was a man called Boris Johnson. Before he was elected to run the country on 24th July 2019, he had been a journalist and a politician. Where he lived at No. 10 Downing Street in London, so too did a cat by the name of Larry. I don't know who gave the cat a name which would have been more befitting a lamb, but Larry was employed by the Cabinet Office in the same way as the government officials were, although their recruitment criteria were somewhat different of course.

Larry was given the title of Chief Mouser, and he

quickly fitted into his 'meet and greet' role after being rescued from Battersea Dog and Cat Home – funnily enough, the same place where your great granddad and I got Cassie, our pet black Labrador, back in the 80s. Having made himself at home pretty quickly, the brown and white tabby soon became lazy at his job and it was only by the skin of his teeth that he managed not to get fired after he ignored a mouse that had been seen running around the previous Prime Minister's study – or so the story goes.

Talking of stories, you've heard of Dick Whittington, right? Now just as Mr Johnson had been Mayor of London before he got elected as Prime Minister, so too Dick had assumed that title some 800 years earlier. He too had a cat, which was given the title of Chief Pest Controller, and rumour has it he was called Tommy, although, again, no one ever knew for sure.

Now despite the fact that Dick never actually got to live at No. 10, *his* cat had much more responsibility than Larry and respectably saw off thousands of rats that were roaming the streets of London at a time when the Bubonic Plague was hitting the headlines, leading to the Black Death in the fourteenth century – an infectious disease where the onset of illness was between 1-7 days after exposure, not unlike the coronavirus.

High up on a hill in an area of London called the Archway is a place called Highgate Hill. There stands a hospital called the Whittington, where a monumental stone (the Whittington Stone) lies at the front of the building and perched on top is a stone statue of Tommy, honoured in his own right.

It is the hospital, incidentally, where all your great aunt and uncles were born at Muswell Hill, whereas I, on the other hand, was born elsewhere.

Moving on then...

It was on the 24th March 2020 that Prime Minister Johnson stood outside his house once again, but this time it was to announce that the UK was about to go into 'lockdown' – a term that we were not familiar with, so we had no idea what it would entail. Our leader had no option but to take urgent action to prevent the spread of infection after so many people in the UK had died from the virus, and he insisted that a national lockdown was the easiest and safest way to help manage the situation to minimise the risk of future deaths.

It was not a decision he had taken lightly. What about work? What about schools? What about shopping? Will I be able to go out to church? What happens if I run out of medicines? Those were just some of the many questions' folks asked themselves, and panic soon started to set it.

As a nurse, I knew more than ever that my job would be safe, but I did wonder what lay ahead for my patients and my colleagues as well as me and my 'own.' It got me thinking about my own history lessons at school – about the Second World War mainly – if only for the simple reason that every single day that it lasted, the uncertainty of what tomorrow would bring had hung over people's heads for six years, wondering if things would *ever* get back to normal.

But how did the two situations compare? I mean, *really?*

Now let's see. At a little earlier than one-thirty in the afternoon on the 3rd September 1939, the then Prime Minister, Mr Neville Chamberlain, gave an address to the nation which was somewhat different from Boris'. He declared that Britain was at war with Germany.

'Public enemy number one' was a term that the government used to describe Adolf Hitler – the leader of Germany – after he had started to kill people indiscriminately during the conflict, and with the coronavirus being identified as an 'invisible' agent not to be reckoned with either, they were considered equally dangerous.

Since the year dot, germs of any kind have always had the potential to kill, yet the coronavirus somehow heightened the need for people to take infection control precautions more seriously than ever before.

Thankfully, things had come a long way since the 1920s. Back then, people would spit in the streets, drink from each other's glasses and pass cigarettes around – all considered to be 'normal behaviour' – and the word 'cross-infection' had yet to be invented. The thought of this happening during the pandemic was horrifying.

When I was growing up there were two particular diseases around which were highly contagious, diphtheria and scarlet fever, and anyone who had them automatically used their common sense and stayed indoors so as not to pass the infection on to others. During that era there were no proper chemists around or special telephone helplines like NHS 111 – 'alive' during and before the coronavirus pandemic – and the 1920s doctors used to make medicines up themselves using all sorts of ingredients (mainly herbs and other plants).

One plant in particular, called digitalis, was highly poisonous and if given in the wrong doses could prove fatal, and yet the purple flowers with bell-like petals were beautiful, which just goes to prove you should never judge a book by its cover. My mum used to refer to that plant by its common name, foxglove, and as youngsters my siblings and I were deterred from picking that as much as touching the deadly nightshade plant, for the same reason.

There was no 'wonder drug' for diphtheria, or scarlet fever for that matter, and the only advice doctors could give the parents of affected children was to 'let nature take its course' – in other words, hope for the best.

Like the coronavirus, the main symptoms were an exceedingly high temperature and a pneumonia-type illness and hundreds of children died from respiratory failure as a result. Luckily for us my parents had the common sense to get us all inoculated against these diseases as well as whooping cough, tetanus and polio.

There was absolutely no cure for polio, a serious viral infection that had the potential to cause temporary or permanent paralysis, whereas tetanus (or 'lockjaw' as mum called it) was a bacterial infection that caused breathing problems in the same way as Covid-19.

With Guillain Barré syndrome rumoured to be a condition that quite often sets in within eight weeks of getting a tetanus vaccination, I had to consider myself something of a late developer, as it was not until I reached the age of 45 that my body started to fight this unexplained infection that had come on without warning, leaving me weak and paralysed for a significant period of time. However, I was lucky, and I got better eventually.

For me then, the coronavirus at the time seemed little more than all those old-type illnesses rolled into one with the common denominators of a high fever, dry cough and shortness of breath and a condition that you either got over or you didn't.

Anyway, by 11th April 2020 the people of the UK were all to stay at home and go out only if absolutely necessary, such as to work if unable to do so from home, to go shopping only for 'essential' items and to take only one form of outside exercise a day if necessary like walking the dog, and not to stray too far, making sure to stay at least two metres apart from anyone else in the process.

Fearful that the supermarkets might suddenly close or they not be able to go out at all, people took to panic buying and stockpiling essential items such as toilet roll, and I witnessed some hilarious scenes of hysterical greed at my local store, I can tell you, as it became the most sought-after item of all time. It had become a case of every man (or woman) for him/herself and there was no consideration for others as that and other things, like sugar and flour, flew off the shelves.

Considering the death toll from the coronavirus was rapidly rising, no one seemed to take a blind bit of notice at that point, or of the need to maintain a safe social distance from others. Mass gatherings in the supermarkets got the PM thinking about other places where the virus could easily be spread, which led him to make a further emergency announcement upon which pubs, restaurants, theatres, gyms, hotels, places of worship and non-essential shops like car showrooms were then forced to close with immediate effect. The word 'lockdown' was now starting to mean exactly what it said on the tin. (Ask your folks what I mean by that)!

It was the restaurant closures that came as the biggest blow to me, as eating out was one of my greatest thrills in life, along with being able to add to my collection of souvenir menus.

The rule on 'essential travel' meant that the weekend that your Great Aunt Lisa had planned for us had to go amiss and I was so looking forward to having afternoon tea at the Ritz again and possibly even the Savoy – an even 'swankier' hotel, so I was led to believe.

Whilst it seemed a great sacrifice at the time, I also thought of all those people who had lost their lives at that point and tried to remain optimistic for a new 'tomorrow.' But tragic as things were, I thought surely nothing could ever compare to the 70,000 civilians' lives that were lost during the Second World War in addition to those of almost 400,000 soldiers, although the circumstances were totally different.

CHAPTER 7

TALES FROM THE UNDERGROUND

When your Great-Great-Nanny Mabel and your Great-Great-Granddad Robert were busy surviving World War Two, the high-pitched sound of the sirens was something they learned to live with. It warned them that enemy planes were about to fly overhead, the opposition being intent on dropping their bombs on London town to kill as many people as they could.

Thick white lines had been painted on kerbs and lamp posts in the streets so that when the streetlights had to be temporarily put out to make it harder for the enemy to see their target, people could still see where they were going, and it helped to prevent accidents from cars piling on top of each other.

With underground tunnels considered to be the safest place of all during an air raid, the risk of catching coughs or colds from strangers mingling together was a chance people took, as it beat getting blown up instead.

Kids in particular had absolutely none of the sneezing or coughing etiquette they do today, which only helped facilitate the spread of germs, especially when sleeping virtually side by side in make-shift hammocks tied to the walls above the train tracks which had become common place.

People's social lives were sacrificed, as families were reluctant to go out unless absolutely necessary for fear of being bombed. The only real source of entertainment they had to keep them in touch with what was going on in the wider world was listening to the news on the radio (the wireless as it was called then) to learn about what the troops were up to on the frontline and praying that the postman wouldn't come knocking on their doors with a telegram to say that their loved ones had been killed in action.

A young woman by the name of Vera Lynn, nicknamed the 'Forces Sweetheart', soon became a household name through singing at outdoor concerts for the troops at the heart of the fighting. You must have heard her most famous song, 'We'll Meet Again'. Having to shield herself during the coronavirus lockdown on account of her age by then – she was 103 – she sang it from her home to mark the 75th anniversary of VE Day on the 8th March 2020 as a 'symbol of hope' (as was considered by all) to help lift our spirits as the pandemic took hold. Sadly, she died just three months later.

The celebrations that would ordinarily have taken place each year could not go ahead, although the Red Arrows still took to the skies and Her Majesty the Queen gave a speech to the nation about 'never giving up or despairing' and recalling her own experiences of WW2.

Whilst it was the men who had done most of the fighting in WW2, so too had many women been conscripted into the Army, Navy or Air Force to 'do their bit,' and those who did not meet the sign-up criteria volunteered to become part of what had become known as the 'Land Army' to provide support a little closer to home. Those willing participants helped to keep the food chain going by working on the farms and picking crops in the fields which would otherwise have gone rotten, and their efforts enabled businesses to stay afloat financially.

To make it fair on everyone, the wartime Government brought in rationing, which provided equal opportunity for people to get hold of the basic food items they needed to survive during that time of crisis. Not all items were rationed however, just the more hard- to -come by ones such as bacon, ham, butter, meat, tea, lard, cheese, eggs, jam and sweets. There was a limit to how much people could have at any one time. Upon registering at their local shop, they were coupons, which came in the form of a ration book.

Rationing carried on for a good nine years after the war ended and stopped just a couple of years before I was born. Queuing up for hours on end just to get hold of the 'bare necessities' had almost become a way of life, but funnily enough there was no shortage of toilet roll.

In 1941 a rich businessman called Oliver Lyttleton imposed a rationing on clothing, and as the President of the Board of Trade he had compiled his own speech to the nation during the time of war, although he was not standing in front of No. 10 Downing Street.

'I know all the women will look smart, and we men may look shabby' he said, telling them that if they did, they should not be ashamed but think of it more as becoming 'battle-stained' in that the sacrifices they had made by not wasting money on new clothes contributed in some small way towards the cost of an aeroplane, a gun or a tank. He considered it to be a more honourable 'title' than scruffy.

During the time of the coronavirus then, I considered the UK Prime Minister had unquestionably contributed towards the 'shabby chic' look, for which he himself made no apology. His style was described in the *Financial Times* as being 'scruffy yet artfully choreographed.' Funny how the press had a way of putting a spin on things to make it sound less rude or judgemental.

The year 2020 was not an era when men and women had to go off to war or work the land, and for those who were lucky enough to be able to work from home, the government arranged for 80% of their normal wages to be paid to them through a scheme called 'furloughing'. It was only meant to be for a few months but was extended to almost six.

Being able to spend time with the family and not having to rush to catch the bus or train or negotiate the rush hour by car was welcomed by those who were privileged enough to fall into that category, and with less stress most felt it was worth sacrificing 20% of their normal wages for.

With the schools having closed to all but children of 'keyworkers', such as those who worked in the police, the fire brigade, the National Health Service or any other emergency or essential services, other kids had to take to 'remote' learning, as I will explain as I go along.

The furlough scheme, incidentally, was a far cry from what people could expect in the way of financial support at the time of the Great Depression back in the 1920s when the UK was in such a bad economic state that thousands of people became unemployed. The phrase 'job retention scheme', which in essence was what 'furloughing' was about, was unheard of back then and whilst there was a different type of benefit – called the National Insurance Scheme – available then, it only lasted for six weeks and was only made available to the fortunate few.

The 2020 furlough scheme wasn't means-tested, but under the National Insurance Scheme workers had to undergo a vigorous investigation by the authorities, and it was only after they could be satisfied that the person had pawned anything they had of any value that they were given 'tickets' entitling them to bread, margarine, tea and sugar only. The assessors even went so far as to check under the person's Lino (vinyl lay, to you) to make sure they did not have any money hidden underneath. Can you imagine that?

Fortunately for families on low incomes or on benefits during Covid-19, they did not have to endure such scrutiny as the Government sent out food vouchers to them to the value of £15 per child, per week, to spend at designated supermarkets. Just like the furlough scheme which, as I said, was only meant to run for a set period of time, so too those school vouchers were only meant to be available for six weeks, but then a young footballer who played for Manchester United F.C. won a campaign for it to be extended until the end of the school summer holidays after recalling his own experiences of having free school dinners as a child before he made the big time.

Certain supermarkets across the country thought they would do their bit to help the NHS staff by opening their stores earlier than usual and setting aside 'protected' time for them to shop as a 'thank you' for their effort to help save lives, yet many NHS employees were administrative or ancillary staff who had no direct contact with Covid-19 patients. They were still considered to be 'local heroes' compared to nursing home staff.

After a huge outcry by non-NHS workers this

courtesy was finally extended to community health workers, who were working under the same stressful conditions as those in the hospital settings yet were grossly undervalued in the public eye.

I deliberately chose not to see that protected time as something to be thankful for, even though I was fully entitled to take advantage of it. Why, I thought, would I want to be in a line-up with the very people who had been at the forefront of nursing the sickest of people with coronavirus – whether standing two metres apart from me in the queue or not – when I could go and shop on any quiet day of the week when I was off work and feel far safer around 'normal' shoppers who, in most cases, would have been taking social isolating and social distancing very seriously and only venturing out now and then, much like myself, in order to feed the family?

Critical thinking had always been at the heart of everything I had been taught during my own training, so all I was doing was putting theory into practice!

There was a time when it was starting to look like there would be more sick people than beds available in the hospitals, and it was amazing how quickly the government commissioned the building trade to knock up several new hospitals to cope with any 'overspill', yet there had been a shortage of social housing for many years before that. Those new builds became known as the Nightingale hospitals.

Within the armed forces there are what's known as 'reservists' – that is, those people who are not part of the regular Army, Navy or Air Force but give up their time a few evenings a week to do similar training so as to be able to provide back-up in an emergency situation.

I have no doubt that you have been reading the story about how your great-granddad and I met, which was at a place in Worship Street in London when we ourselves were army reservists back in 1975. It was a chance meeting which began a love that was to last a lifetime but for the events that unfolded, hence my story today.

Your Great-Grandad lived in Sussex and I in North London and we used to meet at the headquarters on Tuesday and Thursday evenings for a couple of hours at a time. We fell in love pretty much at first sight, were engaged three months later and married in 1977.

I can still recall the panic that set in when I got my mobilisation papers through the post when I was still living at home. I thought it meant that I had to go off to 'fight' there and then alongside the regular army or on other military operations, and it was only then that it hit home to me exactly what I had signed up for.

Your great-granddad used to tease me all the time about how I had got it so wrong, but having left the TA before we got married being sent away and separated was not something we needed to worry about after that.

The relevance of my time spent there will soon become apparent.

Now with the coronavirus being highly contagious, nursing and medical staff caring for sick patients the world over had to wear special enhanced personal protective equipment which included a full-length waterproof gown, gloves, goggles, masks and face shields. Looking at them all 'geared up' reminded me of the time your great-granddad and I had to go into a gas chamber as part of our nuclear, biological and chemical training at the TA. Instead of a blue disposable gown we had to don a white all-in-one suit which was better known as a 'Noddy suit' as the hood was pointed, much like that worn by a character called Noddy created by the previously-mentioned author Enid Blyton, although our hoods did not have silver bells on the end of them.

Anyway, the NBC suit was something that we had to wear over our regular uniform during our time in the chamber, and although it was only a 'mock' exercise, in time of war we might have found ourselves having to wear it for days on end to protect against any radioactive material or in some case, radiation.

The gas chamber was basically a room full of tear gas (an irritant), and unless our masks were put on properly, we were at risk of sneezing, coughing or tearing, and just like the symptoms of the coronavirus our eyes, nose, mouth and lungs would have become affected and made us feel sick.

Now, with potentially more patients than staff to manage the pandemic as of April/May 2020, the Government started writing to ex-medical staff to ask them to consider coming out of retirement and back into the 'system' as extra pairs of much-needed hands.

'Oh, what a good idea', you might be thinking, but when I heard of this plan, I wasn't so sure. When considering those who may have been out of the profession for donkey's years, I got to thinking, would I eat a yogurt that was past its sell-by date? Would I eat it and see what happened, or would I simply bin it and not want to take the risk with my health? I subsequently thought that surely those people would have been 'best before' they retired.

At peak quality, I thought, it might still have been safe to consume a yogurt after its best-before date, but there was a good chance that the flavour and texture would have started to deteriorate.

As a consumer I would have been in charge of making my own judgment about whether to eat or get rid of the possibly contaminated substance, but as a passive receiver of care would I be prepared to put my trust in someone who had been out of practice so long that they might not have been given an update on how to put a suppository in correctly? By that I mean bullet end first and not the other way around, as I was once taught whilst still observing nurses from the older generation doing the exact opposite some 16 years later.

I had already made it clear to everyone around me that should I become ill as a result of the virus on no account was I to be admitted to the No Hope Saloon but instead I should be left to die in my own bed in my own home with family by my side. I had your great-granddad's death at an NHS hospital to thank for that decision.

I had read an article in *The Guardian* – yet another publication that may have faded into oblivion by the time you read this – which stated that one elderly retired nurse, having received a letter to ask if she would be willing to return to the profession during the pandemic, reportedly said that she would rather shove a rusty six-ich nail up her backside than return to her old job. Well, if that was supposed to offer reassurance to the general public, I thought to myself, then I am a Dutch uncle!

As a complete movie buff and always on the lookout for ways I could incorporate humour into my writing, I started to wonder why, if the NHS is was so desperate for staff, the Health Minister had not considered ringing up Dr Kildare, Dr Zhivago, Dr 'beam-me-up Scotty' McCoy, Dr Frankenstein, Doc Brown (who could go back to the time before the virus hit us and use it in his future work) or Patch Adams on their behalf, although it would have been quite likely that this chap's infectious hilarity would have penetrated even the best PPE.

Sadly, most of the stars from the *Carry on Doctor* and *Carry on Nurse* 'films were no longer alive by now – only two cast members were left, Jim Dale, who was 84 years old, and Barbara Windsor, who was pushing 83. She had been diagnosed with dementia a few years earlier and so could not fully understand what lockdown and social distancing meant when none of her friends had popped it to see her at home as before. Either way they were too old to be dragged out of retirement and were part of the 'shielding' programme. There was no script that could have covered the seriousness of it all and combined it with humour when real people were dying every day.

CHAPTER 8

AIR (ON THE SIDE OF CAUTION)

Boy, was I glad I was not in my final year as a student nurse when the pandemic hit the streets! I most certainly would not have considered it a 'positive experience' to be recruited even before taking my final exam to provide support to the medical and nursing staff as part of major hospital responses to Covid-19, as was happening when the NHS found itself stretched to the limit.

My medical placement as a 2nd year student was on a respiratory ward and I remember how nervous I was as I shadowed my mentor in her day-to-day management of patients with anything from asthma, bronchitis and chronic obstructive airway disease (COAD) as it was called at the start of the Millennium (the 'airway' bit was later replaced with 'pulmonary', as in COPD).

The patients' ages varied greatly and one of the things I always found hard to understand was how they got to be diagnosed with 'hospital-acquired pneumonia'. Surely the point of going into hospital was to get better, not to end up with something you would not have got in the first place had you stayed away.

Whilst on placement I was allowed to get involved in the aftercare of a tracheostomy in relation to wound care, but I was not expected to do any airway 'clearance' such as suctioning or administering oxygen flow rates through a mask. I was only able to change a nasal cannula where the rate of oxygen was already set by the qualified nurse, as these were potentially harmful interventions.

I was very keen to follow the Rules of Study, as my biggest fear was always that I might have got confused by the two flowmeters on the wall behind the hospital beds, which at first glance looked the same, and that in a state of panic I could have given a patient air instead of oxygen and found myself up on a charge of manslaughter before my career had even taken off.

I remember during my time on placement hearing the word 'septicaemia', which was explained to me, in simplistic terms, as blood poisoning. So naïve was I then that I thought all the nurses needed to do was to flush the poison out of the patient's system by giving them lots of fluids to dilute the 'bug' and that would be that.

There was no such thing as a sepsis pathway back in 2000, but by the time your Great Grandad was in hospital twelve years later the clinicians should have known exactly how to manage such a condition. Unfortunately, they had failed to do so. I could not understand how the NHS had managed to persuade student nurses in their final year that 'helping out' on Covid-19 wards would be a great experience for them. It meant allowing many who were technically unqualified at that point to treat patients with this life-threatening illness, putting themselves at risk.

I felt sure that for many medical or nursing staff who had returned to the hospitals during the pandemic to 'help out' their intentions were honourable, but I was still finding it hard to forgive and forget those who had let your Great-Granddad down, and I could not bring myself to be one of the thousands of people across the country who used to stand on their doorsteps every Thursday for weeks on end to clap the NHS workers on the 'front line'.

My neighbours knew I was a nurse – they saw me go off to work every day in uniform, not knowing whether it would be in a hospital or other care setting – yet no one ever came out to clap me, nor should I have wanted them to, as I was simply doing my job. I was equally on the front line, if not in front of the cameras, when having to care for those who had acquired Covid-19 and to protect others from getting it, people who were already living with dementia or the aftermath of a stroke or already nearing the end of their lives.

I found the whole clapping thing quite hypocritical, considering no one seemed to give two hoots about their neighbours before it started to get televised and once this stopped, they all went back into hibernation.

I had to feel more sympathy for the 1950s housewives who quite often only got to see their neighbours once a week in any case – usually on a Monday morning when they embarked on a bit of donkey stoning, which meant cleaning their front door steps with a chalky-white brick dipped in water. They would seize the opportunity to exchange gossip as they went about their wifely duties.

My Thursday evenings were far better spent catching up with Dr Ranj, whose children's TV programme I played back on my planner. He was a real doctor who used puppets as patients and taught children about different ailments while singing a simple song to help them take their minds of being ill: BE HAPPY, BE HEALTHY, GET WELL SOON.

It was not a slogan I ever expected to show up on the front of the Prime Minister's podium or those of any of his advisers for that matter, nor did it, but I found the thought quite amusing. It really would not have gone down well, especially with those who had lost loved ones from coronavirus already or those who were recovering from it – far from happy, far from healthy and hopeful that they would get well sooner rather than later.

CHAPTER 9

A TEST IN TIME

Now it wasn't just NHS staff that the Government had advertised for to help out around the country but ex-army reservists who were being called upon to assist with coronavirus testing after several testing stations had been set up across the country. Those volunteers may not have been on the front line of care like returning healthcare workers, but they were at the front line of people's throats and nasal passages, having been given the boring task of swabbing them in a factory-like manner.

What I found highly amusing was that they were expected to undertake training first in the donning and taking off of non-sterile gloves, a plastic apron and a face shield, yet, just as I had been, they were trained in the use of a gas mask and wearing an NBC suit!

Likewise those volunteers had to been given training in the 'art' of swabbing, and whilst it might sound as if I was 'dissing' my ex-companions, to be fair, the task of sticking a long-handled stick with a cotton bud on the end down someone's gullet and up their noses could have been performed by a trained monkey and a lot more cheaply, considering people with no training whatsoever had taken to ordering home test kits such as I had at the start of the pandemic.

I was somewhat bemused therefore by the ten-page instruction leaflet that came with my sampling pack, and considered I would have got far less information to work with had I been about to put together some flat-packed furniture.

Amusingly, I set to compare the two things. As with any 'flat-packs' I had ordered in the past, my first step was to check that my 'Covid' kit contained all the things I needed with which to get going. It took me a matter of seconds, and the fact that the pack was missing screws, bolts, dowels and an Allen key was of no consequence to me.

One Instruction booklet; one sheet of barcode labels (4 labels); one Royal Mail return label; one zip-lock plastic bag containing a swab inside a sealed wrapper and a plastic vial containing a small amount of liquid; one sheet of absorbent material; one biohazard bag with a silver seal and the return box. All present and correct.

I set about following the instructions to the letter, just as I would have done if I were about to rig up a set of chest of drawers, going through each step methodically and making sure I put the right thing in the right place at the right time. It was not unlike doing my medication round, except that my focus was more on making sure I had the right patient, that they were given the right dose and that it was given in the right quantity, by the right route and at the right time.

Luckily, I did not need to have a Stanley knife or any type of screwdriver on standby. The only tool that might have proved useful, as the instruction leaflet suggested, was a mirror to help me see the inside of my mouth when trying to locate my tonsils. I for one did not consider this at all necessary, as I felt confident that I would be able to locate them in the usual place.

Nowhere on a DIY leaflet would it recommend that the customer blow their nose and cough into a tissue before tackling the job, though in this instance I could see the logic.

No sooner had the kit arrived than I booked the free courier collection online as instructed – it would be anywhere between 8am and 4pm the following day, having taken notice of the fact that the swab test needed to be carried out between 9pm on the day of arrival and 7am the following morning.

Having read the instruction leaflet thoroughly and learning that the test kits were 'time sensitive' and expired after 48 hours of the swab being taken, I didn't have to be a genius to know that the later it was done the better. I was also bearing in mind that I might not necessarily be the first 'pick-up', and that it still needed to make the journey to the test centre, of which no one seemed to know the whereabouts. Anyone would think it were at some secret headquarters, like in a James Bond film.

Anyway, as always I got up at the crack of dawn and with eyes barely opened, I fumbled around the keyboard on my laptop trying to register my kit online using the details from one of the four barcode stickers that came with the kit. I then sat poised with my mobile phone in hand, waiting for a text message from the Covid-19 test centre to come through so that I could complete the registration, else they would not have known where to text or email me my result.

Registration completed, I then set about washing my hands for 20 seconds (or so) whilst humming 'happy birthday' in my head – suggested by health organisations as a good length of time to wash them to reduce the spread of infection. Having cleared my nose and throat as instructed I first poked the cotton stick around my tonsils and down my gullet for a count of ten seconds (or so) gagging all the while.

There was something psychologically disturbing about having to put the swab stick I had just removed from my throat up my nostrils, again rotating it for 10-15 seconds before slowly removing it and placing it into the plastic bottle tip end down (of course), but this I did. Then I snapped the end of the stick off, making sure it was fully submerged in the small amount of liquid in the bottom of the vial before screwing the lid on tightly.

It was then just a matter of rolling the container onto the piece of absorbent paper and placing it in the biohazard bag with a silver seal (not real silver you understand) and making sure that a second barcode matched the one on the outside of the specimen pot. Almost finished.

Not having a black belt in origami, and conscious that time was ticking away, I wondered if I would ever master the art of putting the return box together, but when I finally put the biohazard bag inside and closed it using the security seal I thought – finally I can get on and enjoy my early morning cuppa. I prayed I would not have to go through that ordeal ever again.

It had made no difference to me what time of day the courier arrived as I had already chosen to take a few days off work because I just hadn't felt 'right', hence the reason why I had chosen to self-isolate in the first place. Half my work colleagues had already gone off 'sick' by that time, fearful that they might become victims, which left me to cover extra-long shifts on days I would not ordinarily have been working and with no recommended face protection at that time.

The courier knocked on the door and quickly moved away from me as I opened it. I placed the cardboard pouch on the front lawn and stood back in my hallway to allow him to pick it up. I couldn't help blurting out: 'It's OK – it's not about to explode.'

Well, at least he saw the funny side of it. What I

found funny was that he had parked his car at the end of a neighbour's driveway, having left the doors wide open with someone else in the driving seat as if they were in a getaway car.

I left it a while before setting about tracking my package's journey to the test centre, having been methodical enough to write down the barcode from the Royal Mail 24-hour tracking label before letting it go. I remained convinced that the test centres were in secret locations since I was not able to track my parcel after it arrived at the regional distribution centre. All I could do after that was wait.

The result of putting together a chest of drawers would have been instantly obvious – either the job had been done successfully or not – but the nail-biting wait to see if I had acquired the virus or not was something else. I did not expect to test positive, so the news that I had it came as a complete shock to me. and I was only pleased that I had followed the rules on not allowing anyone, not even my family, into the house in the weeks before. I had none of the 'normal' symptoms except for a very slight temperature on my last day at work, although I had wondered why my food had not tasted 'quite right' for a day or two before and why I could no longer smell my perfume. I most certainly had not linked the two.

So now I had to officially self-isolate for a further seven days, and had it not been for my then wanting to find out how the virus might affect me, I would never have stumbled upon the many articles on line that suggested my symptoms were the 'hidden' ones that were yet to be proven to have a link to Covid-19. I felt hopeful that once the bug was out of my system my taste buds and sense of smell would go back to normal and that everything would stop smelling and tasting like metal. In the meantime, I had to contend with cooking for the sake of keeping my immune system going to help fight any underlying infection, as opposed to being able to get any pleasure from eating. I added extra chillies to my home-made curries, but that did nothing to satisfy me.

I was not to know at that point that on return to work I should be given the task of helping my staff to get tested, but I was happy to guide them through the process. If only I had kept my WRAC uniform from 1975 I would have asked permission from my manager to wear it instead of my navy blue one so that I could have 'felt the part', if only to see the reaction on my colleagues' faces, as they had no idea that I had ever been in military service.

After helping with over 25 swabs (and that was just the staff) I had become a dab hand at making up the postage boxes if nothing else and felt particularly productive that day.

CHAPTER 10

THE OYSTERS WENT A.W.O.L

At the start of the pandemic the Prime Minister had described the coronavirus as 'the worst public health crisis for a generation.' More so than the Ebola outbreak of 2014 or the Zika Virus of 2016, I thought to myself? Or the Spanish flu that had swept the world in the aftermath of World War One, resulting in over a hundred million deaths from a pneumonia-type illness not dissimilar to Covid-19?

Everyone thought they had it tough during this pandemic, but unlike in wartime our men didn't have to resort to using bicarbonate of soda as a substitute for an antiperspirant and our women did not have to use soot from chimneys as eyeshadow, or gravy browning on their legs to resemble stockings, and then drawing a seam down the back with a black pen to add a little sexiness. People didn't have to resort to eating poor knights' fritters – sandwiches made from bread spread with margarine, jam, golden syrup or fruit, then cut into fingers and fried in hot fat. They would have tasted nicer if the sandwich fingers had first been dipped into beaten reconstituted dried egg and mixed with a little milk before frying, then topped with sugar afterwards.

Nor did they have to take to eating mock oyster soup, a recipe that contained no oysters whatsoever but was instead made up of fish trimmings, artichokes, onions or leeks flavoured with mace, mixed herbs, white peppercorns and parsley. It was boiled in a mixture of water and milk with a clove thrown in for good measure. No one had to settle for eating mock oyster pudding either, which equally contained no oysters but fish roes as a substitute. When mixed with breadcrumbs, milk, reconstituted dried eggs and sugar and nutmeg it required being baked in a moderate oven for 30 minutes until golden brown.

I couldn't think of any two dishes that were more bland, but that is what rationing meant during time of war – people making do with what they had – and tinned snoek (a type of mackerel that was imported from South Africa) would have been enough to turn anyone vegan!

'We'll eat again, don't know where, don't know when, but I know we'll eat again some sunny day...'

Oh how tempting it was during the pandemic to create my own YouTube channel and recreate that famous Vera Lynn song if only to help uplift the spirits of all those who had felt deprived at not being able to order a take-away once the lockdown measures had fully kicked in.

Talking of the Second Word War got me thinking that whilst Britain had once welcomed the descent of GIs upon our shores to help us out, the last thing we wanted during the pandemic was for anyone from the good old US of A to come anywhere near the White Cliffs of Dover, given that America had boasted the highest death rate than anywhere else from the word go.

The Yanks' attractive uniforms and endless supply of silk stockings and chocolates may have turned the heads of many a UK housewife back in the 40s, but now it was time for them to remain overpaid, oversexed and over there. Besides, social distancing rules put paid to couples from different households being able to get together, so it was not easy to charm each other, let alone get the pants off them, and certainly not from two metres.

When the Prime Minister announced that schools, colleges and universities were to be closed as part of the lockdown measures the kids rejoiced, but then after the initial shock wore off it was left to their parents to do 'home schooling', which did not go down too well since most of them had forgotten what they had learned from their own schooldays.

Teachers did their best to create virtual classrooms to help kids carry on with their lessons as best they could from the other side of their laptops, but still there were those parents who thought it a cheek that they should have to partake at all and kept drumming on about the damage missed schooling was doing to their children's mental health.

Mental health my foot! I mean, it wasn't as if the schools had been damaged during a bombing raid or the Boy Scout or Girl Guide movements would have expected schoolkids to get involved in salvaging war materials and selling them to raise money for munitions as part of the war effort whilst their education suffered. Oh no!

Those 21st century kids had the freedom to spend every waking minute on their Xboxes or other gaming devices and were forced to do just a certain amount of online homework in between times. Just ask your cousins about that because they thought it was 'ace.'

CHAPTER 11

PIGGIN' AWFUL

No sooner had the Prime Minister allowed beaches to be opened up after a period of closure than a 'major incident' was declared at Bournemouth beach as people flocked there like bees round a honeypot, paying no heed to any of the warnings on social distancing and leaving all their litter on the beaches for the locals to clear up afterwards. All that contaminated waste! Yet despite our PM commenting at a press conference the following day that people 'were taking too many liberties', little was done about it or their behaviour.

Now I could have understood if this kind of behaviour had happened during the 1960s, as having to oversee social distancing between the Mods and Rockers would have been challenging for the police. These were the rival gangs who made it a regular weekend 'thing' to get down on the beaches at Margate and Brighton in particular, to kick the cr*p out of each other. Getting arrested was all part of the fun for them but given the potential for far more fatalities from the coronavirus that day in Bournemouth, the few bobbies on the beach had little control over the activities of the mass of beachcombers.

Back in the 50s policemen (I guess I should say police officers now) were respected and feared, but not anymore. Whilst they could have got away with clipping the ear of anyone for having given them little more than a bit of cheek, instead they would have been up on an assault charge way before 2020.

So now, not only had people been 'advised' not to go to their local beaches (not 'forbidden') they were also being deterred from travelling abroad unless it was 'essential'. As more and more countries saw a rise in the death toll, what was considered 'essential' travel was subjective to say the least, and for those people who had chosen to ignore the advice, having to go into 'quarantine' for two weeks after arriving back in the UK did not faze them one little bit.

Yet the government officials had got the word all wrong – what they should have said was that people needed to go into 'self-isolation', since, without a test, those people could not have known for sure whether they had picked up the virus abroad or not. You might be thinking 'come off it, Nanny, it was the same difference', but really it was not.

Seeing on the TV, at the start of the pandemic, hundreds of cruise ship passengers and staff being forced to remain onboard for weeks and weeks pending testing put me off going on a cruise again. I'd had high hopes one day of being able to sail on the largest cruise ship in the world – the *Symphony of the Seas*, courtesy of Royal Caribbean – after seeing a virtual tour of it on the 'box' back in 2018. The ship that your great-great granddad and I had sailed on back in 2012 was spectacular, but this was something else!

Nothing about the coronavirus was predictable. That was the thing.

There were times when if I hadn't laughed, I would have cried. So, laugh I did, but only to myself. I started to wonder – what would Captain Pugwash do if he got stranded on the waters somewhere between China and the UK? He was the captain of a ship called the *Black Pig,* in a popular children's TV programme back in the 70s which my younger siblings used to love watching. Captain P used to claim that he was the bravest buccaneer around, so at the point where Prime Minister Johnson's scientific advisors started telling us that Covid-19 was such a 'sneaky' virus that no one was exempt from getting it, I wondered how this would have affected him and his crew members.

Had any one of them been home to visit *their* folks in recent days I thought? After all, Jonah, the tallest of the captain's 'crew', was from Jamaica and in the weeks before the UK lockdown, although there were only eight cases over there, the Jamaican Prime Minister had declared the island to be a disaster area and was trying hard to contain the spread of the virus. What if Jonah had been one of the eight and had taken it back to the *Black Pig*, I thought, chuckling at the irony of his catchphrase: 'No good will come of this, mark my words.'

Then there was Swine, the Australian pirate who worked for Cut-Throat Jake, Captain Pugwash's arch enemy, who frequently boarded the ship. Australia had already declared 74 deaths as of the 22nd April. Known for always having a mug of grog in his hand, the ship's hand would have done well to stick with it, as hot tea and garlic to treat the virus was nothing more than a myth, and the US President's suggestion that drinking bleach or injecting disinfectant were potential cures for Covid-19 was nothing short of scandalous.

No one could be sure whether Tom the cabin boy – another of the ship's hands – was from the Home Counties or Ireland, but considering the pandemic had reached the Republic of Ireland by the end of February 2020 and within three weeks had spread across all its counties, he could well have been a carrier.

And as for 'simple' Willy from Wigan – the 'thickest' crew member of all – well, Wigan was the town that had one of the sixth highest infection rates in Greater Manchester for a long time.

'Just you wait till we get back to Wigan – we won't half have a tale to tell,' was Willy's signature saying. If only he could have predicted what lay ahead.

So it could have turned out to be a right old tale – an Aussie, a Mexican, a Jamaican, an Irishman, a Mancunian, a Cornishman and even a Scotsman in the form of Captain Scratchwood (Governor and law enforcer for the town of Portobello in Edinburgh – a town that has also not been exempt from getting the virus) – all stuck on a boat together somewhere out at sea with not an inch between them, let alone two metres and face masks!

With a surge in attempts by migrants and refugees to enter the UK by boat during the coronavirus pandemic, I guess that is what made me seek to mess around with a fictitious scenario, although for those real people it was through sheer desperation, and for many it ended up being fatal, thanks to the people traffickers taking advantage of the situation.

Not funny at all!

CHAPTER 12

WHAT CAN'T BE FIXED

I had experienced as much as anyone else not being able to socialise with my family or friends for weeks at the height of the national lockdown and didn't complain about it, but it didn't stop other people from constantly whining about the rules on TV day in and day out. It got tiresome.

It was not as if the bodies or faces of *their* loved ones would have changed beyond all recognition within that short time any more than mine, unlike those who had returned from war, where, for many, their faces would understandably have become redrawn due to their experiences.

At worst, during the pandemic, on account of the barbers being closed, people's hair may have started to resemble bird's nests and their physical appearance generally may have changed depending on whether or not they had sat around doing nothing or had taken to walking up and down their stairs at home as many did, pretending they were climbing the equivalent of Mount Everest in the name of charity or otherwise.

With so many people dying all around, I wanted to shake up the moaning few and say 'think about those who have had their last haircut and will constantly lose weight now that they are six foot under!'

For all my waffling, I guess the point I was trying to make was that over the years people have gone through other very trying times, yet somehow the pandemic had created much more mayhem. Standing shoulder to shoulder with strangers in underground tunnels, sharing toilet seats, following white lines to keep themselves and others safe, having to abide by a fair policy governed by rationing (we were allowed to get away with a joyful free-for-all only after the sweet rationing was lifted in 1953) couldn't have been easy for anyone during the war, yet along came the coronavirus and suddenly everyone considered their lives to be ten times worse. Screechy brakes!

Right kids, if you want to know what happened after that you will have to read my book through to the end, as I am finding it extremely hard to continue to write in the past when this is all still going on around me and likely to be so for the foreseeable future. All I can do from this point onwards is to give you updates as I go along. Even though I cannot distinguish Cabernet from cat's pee right now given that my taste buds have yet to be resurrected, I could really do with a glass of it right now. Either way, the wine must taste better than mock soup, right?

CHAPTER 13

MELANCHOLY BABY

Having taken the opportunity during the 'break' to read back that which I have written, I am instantly aware that the memoir I started out with has taken a bit of a detour. Although I *have* darted around here and there and incorporated into my writing a topic that I never thought possible, my priority must still remain to impart the message that there needs to be a fair justice system for all when things go horribly wrong in hospital.

For so many years my emotional energy has been directed towards what I assuredly value the most – the truth, the basis for my story – despite having thrown in the odd bit of nonsense or two for good measure along the way.

I know it could be said that holding onto resentment is like leaving a knife in a wound, but still I cannot shake it off.

In book 2 (*When Angels Fall*) I poked fun at the tragedy of my husband's loss by setting up an imaginary courtroom in which I could question those I still feel are responsible for his death. Sitting here with nothing better to do right now as I remain in self-isolation, I have had to take a step forward myself, since the law courts have now been forced to close at this time.

For the purpose of my new exercise, I shall call this trial 'Operation Willow Tree', not to be confused with Operation Yewtree of 2012. As a teenager and ardent watcher of 'Top of The Pops', I could never have imagined that the white-haired man with the big neck chain and the even bigger cigar, famous for saying 'now then, now then, guys and girls', would be investigated by the police decades later for matters of turpitude for which he had managed to escape getting locked up, much to the horror of the general public, so there was no way on earth that I was going to contact Jim and ask him to try and fix it for me to get the help I needed to get my case to court as I might otherwise have done back in the 70s had Ted died earlier when his character was seemingly squeaky clean.

Having taken the bull by the horns and emailed the CPS myself in any case I had been literally second's away from pushing the 'send' button.

And then what happened? Along came lockdown.

To echo the words of Humphrey Bogart to the piano player at Rick's Café: 'Of all the towns in all the world,

Covid had to 'walk into' mine.' (*Casablanca* – Warner Bros, 1942.)

Although, to be fair, it was not just my town that got hit but every town from here to kingdom come.

With the police now expected to take on a more active role in enforcing the new health and safety regulations in public by ensuring that society conformed to the rules on social distancing as well as having to make sure law and order was maintained in general, I knew instantly from that point onwards that listening to the ravings of an angry widow would not be on their list of priorities.

Equally I was fully aware that even if I had managed to get someone's attention by chance, with Covid-19 in full swing it would have been impossible for any of the officers to go to the hospital and interview the staff who I had wanted taken to task over hubby's death eight years ago. It does not help that NHS staff were now being hailed as heroes for every person they have managed to save thus far as a result of the virus. Is that not what they are paid to do, in the same way as I am once I can return to work?

Why has this stupid virus rained on my parade?

Anyway, to get back to the matter in hand. Melancholy is how I feel every time I open the mahogany cocktail cabinet upon which the many figurine sculptures that hubby had bought me over the years sit upon the glass shelves. The wooden people with no faces somehow speak to me in a quiet way. Each one tells a story of how they came to be there, when, and in some cases why –

such as for an anniversary, as a Christmas present or following the birth of a child.

In a strange way they give me comfort that he is not far away – in fact, he 'lives' only a stone's throw away, his ashes discreetly displayed in a wooden casket from within a matching unit right next door.

Whether it be called the Angel of Friendship, the Mother and Daughter, or the Promise (don't read too much into that), these loveable works of art have been by my side through thick and thin, looking down at the endless amount of paperwork that has been strewn across my coffee table over the years, paperwork that holds all the evidence I need to work with.

Unlike the Chancellor of the Exchequer in the mid-seventies, the one whose bushy eyebrows became a key feature of impressionist Mike Yarwood's jokes (he who invented the catchphrase 'Silly Billy'), my willow people don't have to worry about getting theirs trimmed or shaped. The same cannot be said for me. I am bordering on a Groucho Marx lookalike, although I *have* managed to keep the top lip under control, thanks to good old Immac. Other hair removal products are available!

Just as Groucho became famous for his wit and wisecracks, so too I have been praised in the same way, although I cannot confess to having got up to any *Monkey Business* (1931) as such, nor have I ever had a liking for *Duck Soup* (1933).

Now I am talking nonsense, but at least I can appreciate when I am being funny but hopefully not to the point of embarrassment, unlike poor Mrs Thatcher – the 'milk-snatcher' – who once announced in public that 'every Prime Minister needs a willy'. She was referring to her loyal and trusted advisor William Whitelaw in some speech or other during her time in office.

It's funny the things people do when they have time on their hands. A few days ago, I bought a share in a racehorse after seeing an 'ad' in one of the national newspapers which I had picked up a few days before I became ill. For a mere £53 I am now a proud part-owner of a sleek, dark brown, five-year-old gelding who goes by the name of Will Carver and is managed by one of the UK's top racehorse trainers. I am so thrilled now that my owner certificate has arrived. I am sincerely hoping for a big win before my registration runs out next year, although I am not holding my breath any more than I should have done if I had had whooping cough as a child!

I have yet to tell my family of my crazy 'indulgence', so keep it a secret for now please.

The last time I was anywhere near a racecourse, it was the one at Alexandra Palace in London where back in the 60s my dad and I would sit in the stands eating monkey nuts. I vividly recall seeing one of the jockeys walk under the belly of one of the bigger horses without even ducking.

Perhaps this is the real reason why I keep getting the words 'furloughed' and 'furlong' mixed up at the moment.

If I hadn't felt so lethargic and reluctant to do anything except lounge around the house in recent days, buying a gee-gee might never have happened, but as my dear old dad used to say: 'You have to speculate to accumulate.' Besides, it took my mind off having to constantly try to work out why a raven is like a writing book, having first read about Alice meeting the Mad Hatter in Wonderland back in 1865.

Well at least I have not taken to putting my iron in the fridge or my watch in the sugar bowl just yet, so the virus couldn't have affected me that badly.

All things considered I have resigned myself to the fact that I must take on the 'operation' myself.

That's fine. I can do it!

Not to be greedy, I shall need to call fourteen 'people', not thirteen, for this jury service, as I do not want to offend anyone by leaving them out. And I shall need to get hold of a perruque – and quickly. It cannot be any old 'wig' – it needs to be brunette of course – and the locks need to be more subtle than is normal, rather like those of the Little Women in Louisa May Alcott's famous novel, else I should ask my nephew Simon if I can borrow his 'real' one.

My wooden friend's legs don't bend, so they will have to stand throughout the hearing and as they do not have a voice-box I shall have to skip the part where ordinarily an oath or affirmation would need to be taken to publicly confirm that they will consider 'faithfully' the issues according to my evidence.

In such a small cabinet it will be difficult to get them to adhere to the social distancing rules, short of having to take them all out, but they *are* a few inches apart and if they are going to transmit anything to each other it is more likely to be canker rot than coronavirus. At least they won't be trying to claim travel money, as they couldn't be any closer to home nor will they be asking to be reimbursed for food and drink, since they do not have any mouths, so that will cut down on court expenses.

Since they don't have 'lugholes' either, it might be a bit difficult for them to hear the evidence, and they won't be able to raise their hands if there is something they have not understood, but I know their eyes will be fixed on my body language and that they will do their best to lip read as I shall refrain from wearing a mask and as for having to keep an open mind – well, that shouldn't be hard since they have hollow heads in any case.

At least I will not have to remind them to turn off their mobile phones during the trial or that note-taking is strictly forbidden as is them communicating anything about the case on Facebook!

'All rise. This court is now in session.'

On second thoughts – this can never work. My fawn and cream friends do not have the capacity to vocalise their decision at the end of the trial, to be able to convey a unanimous guilty verdict, so as head judge I must declare a mistrial and hope that a real-life jury might eventually materialise that will be able to show emotion of some kind and that the outcome will be a good one.

Well, that was a waste of time, wasn't it? At least I now only have an hour to wait until Emmerdale is on. I wonder which of the cast characters they will be focusing on in lockdown this time! I really want Cain and Moira to get back to together and I don't blame Harriet for finding it hard to social distance herself from DI Malone – I would too, because despite being a no-good cop in character, the actor himself definitely has an arresting personality!

CHAPTER 14

STAYING POSITIVE

I think it might help you from now on if I were to add a bit of 'contemporaneousness' to my storyline to make situations and events easier to visualise and connect to as they unfold. Or at least I shall give it a go.

Friday 3rd July 2020

Pubs and restaurants finally get to open tomorrow, but even if my taste buds had returned, and much as I would love to be able to get all 'dolled up' for a night out, I am in no rush to do so all the time there is controlled access to toilets and I must take to pre-booking my meal or ordering food in-house via an app.

I do not relish the thought of having to sit behind a plastic screen and be waited on by someone wearing a mask and told I must stay in my seat unless I am getting up for a good reason (I don't want to have to justify my many trips to the loo), or being permitted to take photographs for my memory book at the risk of snapping outside the yellow and black lines.

I don't want someone taking my temperature before I even set foot in the place – I am the nurse, not them, so I am quite capable of taking my own temperature, and the worse thing of all is that there won't be any fancy menu that I can bring home as a souvenir as I had done from every place I had eaten before this damn virus came along and put paid to the simplest of pleasures.

Instead, through the wonder of cuisine themed TV programmes I have already started to extend my 'bucket list' of places to eat at as soon all bans are lifted, places where I won't have to worry about a face covering clashing with my fur coat.

Sadly my budget won't extend to jet-setting around the world to work my way through the ten most expensive meals money can buy, and I could never justify spending £600 on a burger from an exclusive brasserie in Las Vegas or in neighbouring New York, nor trying sushi that is even more expensive than from one of its top Japanese restaurants given that I am just a nurse and overworked although adequately paid, but it would be wonderful to be able to throw all caution to the wind, as they say. However, I shall be perfectly happy right now just to be able to eat a flame-grilled burger from my local Burger King, whether I can distinguish the taste or not.

Restaurants in New York may well boast of being able to create sundaes that are 'golden and opulent' with a 24-carat gold topping and offer diners the chance to take home the crystal bowls they are served in – but for a thousand quid, that really is pushing the ice-cream boat out.

Pizza, I would say, is my least favourite food, but I must wonder what I might actually get for my ten thousand pounds were I to travel to Salento in Italy and drop in at the Renato Viola restaurant responsible for such indulgence. At the very least I should expect a stuffed crust!

The zillion dollar lobster frittata on offer at yet another New York diner sounds divine although, let's face it, a frittata is little more than a glorified omelette and unless it is made from the geese who laid the golden eggs, I am more than happy to stick to my own home-made Spanish version using bog standard eggs, streaky bacon, peppers, mushrooms, diced potato and a hell of a lot of extra mature grated cheddar on top – started off on the hob then finished off under the grill.

Total cost? Around three quid!

What I wouldn't mind though is the chance to sample the 'multi-sensory experience' that both the Ultraviolet restaurant in Shanghai and the Sublimotion restaurant in Ibiza have to offer, the first with 20 courses and the latter with 15, with projected imagery that changes according to the type of food that is being eaten at the time.

If a memoir is about capturing moments that matter, whether it means jumping back and forth in time or not, whilst the theme may have started out as one thing – the grieving process – writing like this during the Covid-19 crisis has helped bring a lot of detail about what matters most in life and what was important at a specific point in time. It took a positive coronavirus test result to make me appreciate that every moment in life is precious.

The TV's portrayal of the Basque city as Spain's 'culinary capital' however, really got me thinking that perhaps a three-day break there might not be out of the question after all – sometime next year of course, when all the nicer airlines are up and running 'normally.'

HEART IN LOCKDOWN

Camping holiday 1974

Camping holiday 1974

1974 and my dress sense leaves a lot to be desired

HEART IN LOCKDOWN

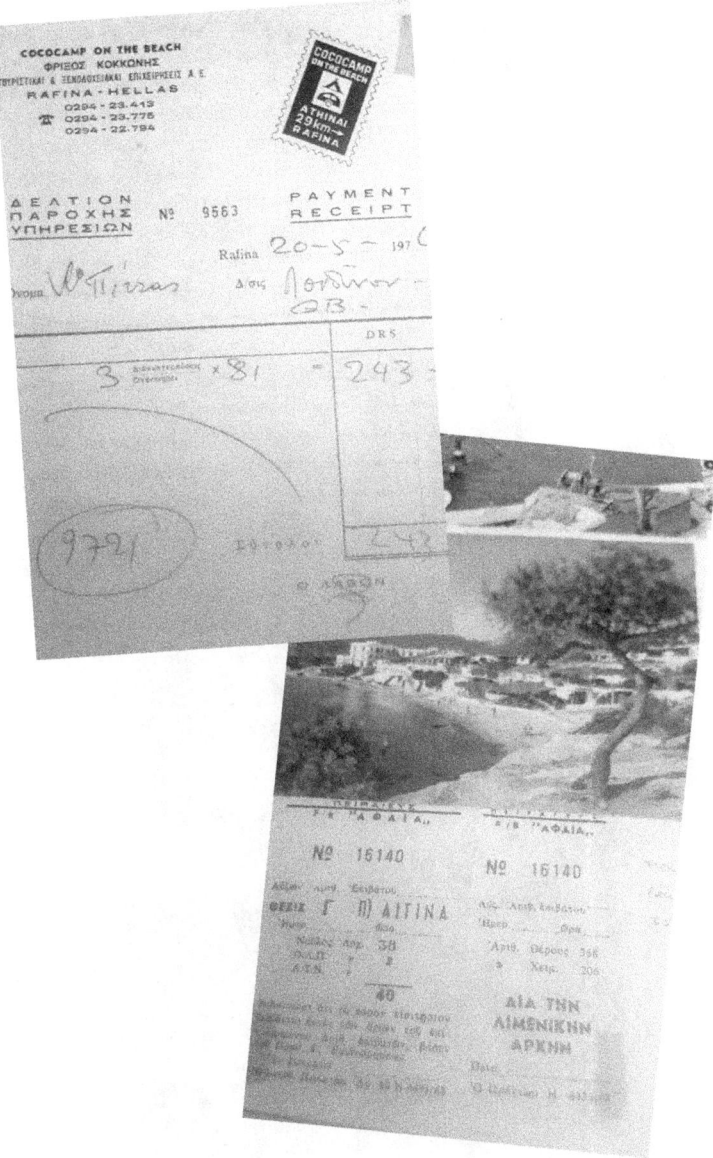

85

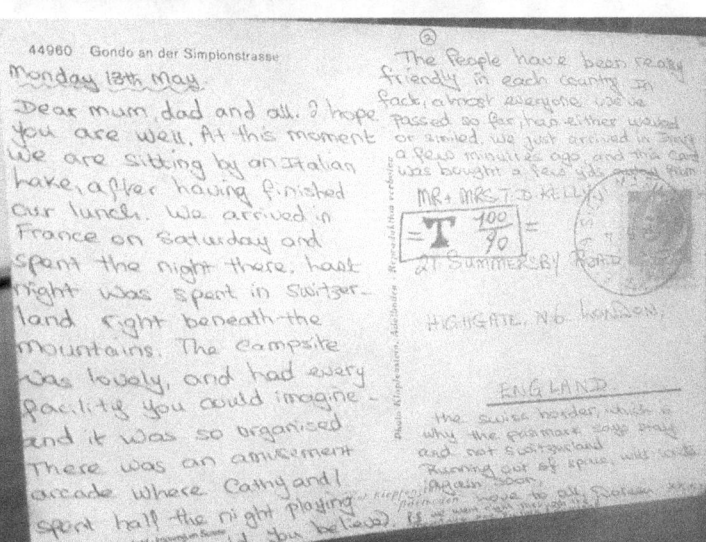

Monday 13th May.

Dear mum, dad and all. I hope you are well. At this moment we are sitting by an Italian lake, after having finished our lunch. We arrived in France on Saturday and spent the night there, last night was spent in Switzerland right beneath the mountains. The campsite was lovely, and had every facility you could imagine — and it was so organised. There was an amusement arcade where Cathy and I spent half the night playing... would you believe...

The people have been really friendly in each country. In fact, almost everyone we've passed so far has either waved or smiled. We just arrived in Italy a few minutes ago and the card was bought a few kids ago from

MR + MRS T.D. KELLY
21 SUMMERSBY ROAD
HIGHGATE, N.6. LONDON.
ENGLAND

the swiss border, which is why the postmark says Italy and not Switzerland. Running out of space, will write again soon.

From here to
eternity

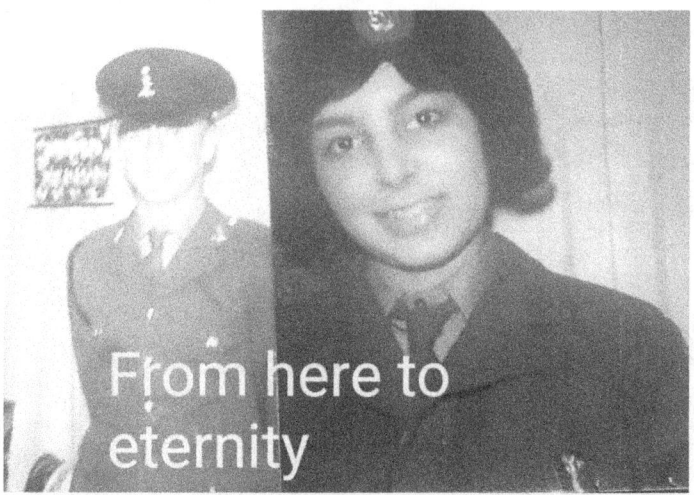

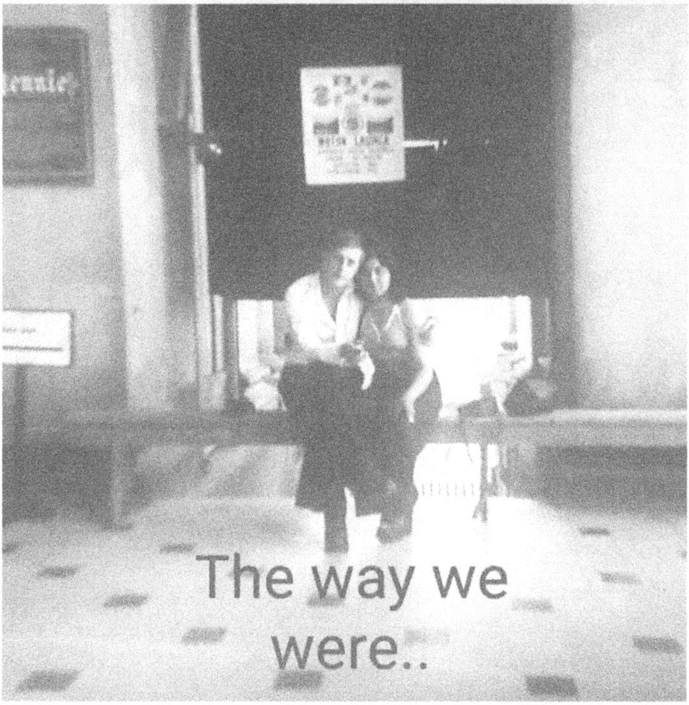
The way we
were..

HEART IN LOCKDOWN

BALMORAL CASTLE

th August, 2020

Dear Mrs Kerry,

The Queen has asked me to thank you for your letter of 21st July from which Her Majesty has noted your further comments regarding the sad death of your husband and your views on his treatment by the National Health Service.

I am afraid I can only reiterate that this is not a matter in which The Queen would become involved, and I am sorry to have to send you another disappointing reply.

While it was kind of you to wish to make Her Majesty aware of the six books you have written, copies of which you enclosed with your letter, I must explain that due to the many similar requests received it is not possible for The Queen to express a view on your work.

Her Majesty is unable to accept your books as gifts and regrettably it is not possible to return unsolicited items.

Nevertheless, it was thoughtful of you to wish to make The Queen aware of your feelings, and I would like to send you my good wishes for the future.

Yours sincerely,

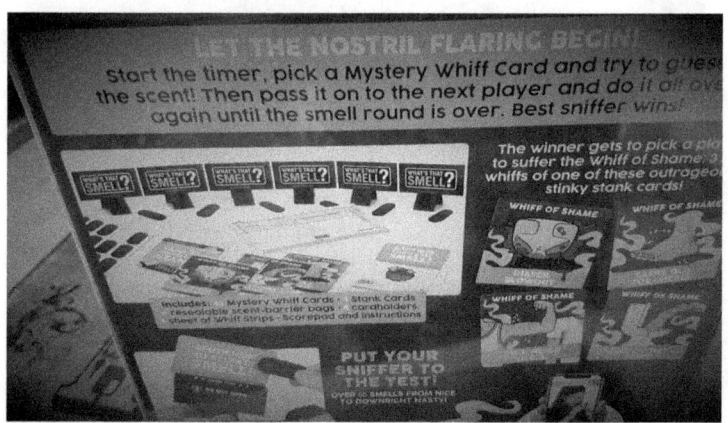

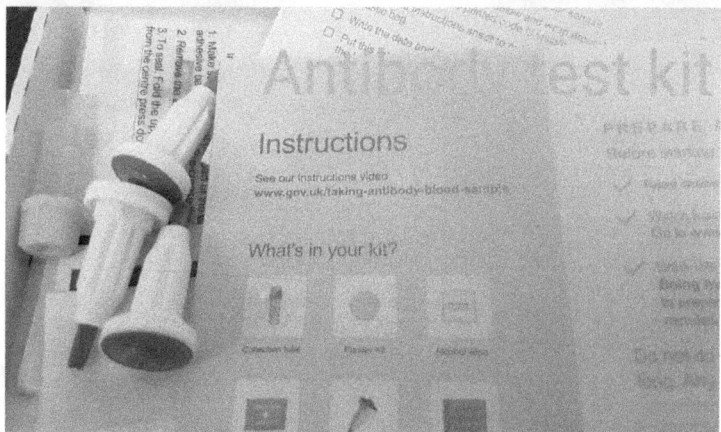

NHS COVID-19 Notification (nhs.covid19.notification@notifications.service.gov.uk)
doreenkerry56@yahoo.co.uk
Tuesday, 5 May 2020, 11:27 BST

Dear DOREEN KERRY

Your Covid-19 test has come back POSITIVE, meaning you have the virus.

You MUST self-isolate for 7 days from the onset of symptoms or from the day of your test if you don't have symptoms. If you develop symptoms you must continue to self-isolate for 7 days from the onset of your symptoms.

All your household members who remain well must stay at home for 14 days from the day you took the test.

For care home staff/residents please follow specific isolation advice for care homes.

You can return to work on day 8 if you have not had a fever in 48 hours, even if you still have a cough. Always contact your employer before returning to work.

For further advice go to https://www.gov.uk/coronavirus.

If your symptoms worsen please go to NHS 111 online, call 111, o dial 999 in an emergency. Sign up for daily recovery support: https://111.nhs.uk/covid-19/sms

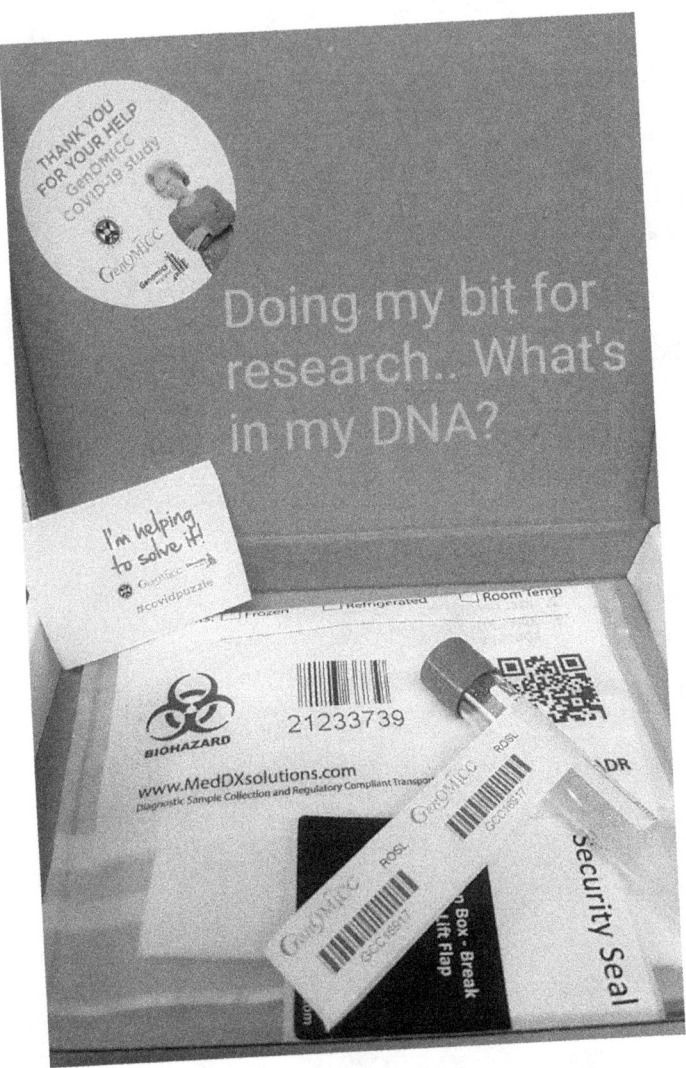

CHAPTER 15

SHUTTLECOCKS GALORE

I don't remember the point where my taste for food and eating out got so 'snobby', but it certainly wasn't the case when I was eighteen or even nineteen, living at home with mum and dad and my six siblings, and grateful for whatever food was put on the table.

Mum and dad never got to eat out much, if at all, and my best friend Cathy and I never really got much further than the local Golden Egg, as I have mentioned in my previous musings. Eating out whilst on holidays abroad with her parents, first in 1974 and then in 1975, most certainly did not extend to Royal tastes.

Perhaps it was coincidence that I dug out yet more of my old diaries from my teenager days shortly before a tour of all things tasty came on the box, which has brought back a promise I made to my bestie a long time ago. 'One day I will write a book about all this', I had told her, never expecting that I would actually get the chance to do so over 45 years later. Given that none of us can know at this point in time whether or not there will be a 'second wave' of coronavirus, now seems as good a time as any to commit to including in my memoirs an account of our three-week trip to Greece when Cathy's dad, who was Greek himself, drove us there and back in his motorhome.

It was on Saturday 11th May 1974 that we took the Seaspeed Hovercraft from Dover to Calais (originally destined for Boulogne) after Cathy's folks picked me up from home early that morning. This was my first ever time away from home. Nor had I ever even been on a camping holiday before, let alone one abroad. The hovercraft was called the *Princess Anne*, and it was just our luck that we had chosen to travel on the same day as a party of school kids.

Having eventually arrived in the north of France we hitched up our igloo tent at a transit camp in Soissons – the other side of Arras, a 75-minute drive away from Calais. We only spent one night there before heading off for Switzerland, stopping at Troyes for lunch. We had 'meat and delicious French loaves' I wrote. I likened Troyes to New York from the buildings and scenery, yet I had never ever been to NY.

We drove through Dijon (best known for its mustard and wine, although I did not know that at the time) before passing over the River Seine, where we stopped for lunch, which consisted of cake, French bread and Swiss cheese, crisps and a drink of Coke.

Having later arrived at the Swiss frontier at a place called Vallorbe, and after being waved on by a customs officer we proceeded to our next campsite in Lausanne, I remember how impressed we were by the facilities at the site, which extended to an amusement arcade, a children's playground, a washing machine, lavatories and a 'very modern' shower! We had not expected a lot, but we had not been thrilled at having to squat over a hole within a dilapidated wooden hut at the last campsite, so we found this much more impressive.

Waking up to the cool Swiss air was quite refreshing, having spent most of the previous evening by a lake amidst the snow-covered mountains. We set off once more after breakfast and drove over the Rhône – one of Europe's biggest rivers – and a couple of hours later we arrived in the German part of Switzerland. We stopped at a place called Visp for tea just before we were about to hit the Great St Bernard Pass.

After that we encountered the Simplon Pass, a motorway high up in the mountains with 22 miles of non-stop bends, which petrified me. Cathy's dad had to carefully negotiate them even though he had a splitting headache by that time. It had been a lot of driving at that point, with a lot more to go.

Having conquered all the death-defying twists and turns we finally arrived in Italy, and after passing through customs again we stopped for lunch near a beautiful lake called Lago Maggiore. An hour later we arrived at the smallest Italian campsite on earth – I described it as no bigger than someone's back garden. After a further night in camp, this time outside the city of Bologna, still in northern Italy, we set off to catch the boat to Greece.

Having driven from the north to the south of the country, we stopped for lunch at a place called Foggia before heading off to the next campsite on the outskirts of Pignolia, which is famous for its Pinot Noir, though I have never been a red wine drinker and certainly didn't drink back in those days in any case.

Finally, the day arrived when we boarded a ferry called the SS *Appia* after a three-hour wait at the Mediterranean dockside. On board I 'fell in love' with Franco, the captain, and decided there and then that I wanted to become a WREN, while Cathy became besotted with a Greek boy called Mikos during our short time on board.

After the ship arrived at Corfu the following morning, we found a campsite at Patras for the night. We had no television and our main entertainment was writing up our diaries and reading – the simplest of pleasures which teenagers of today would sniff at – and we always managed to get chatting with fellow campers, who took a liking to us wherever we went.

The night that followed was spent amidst the neon lights of Athens, which was all lit up against the dark sky with its open-air restaurants along the quay and their waiters all competing for customers. Maybe one day I shall get to go there again as a 'grown up' and the waiters will have to compete for which one serves me first as I make my way through each and every eating house in sight, whilst having to contend with Cathy's mum's cooking in the meantime.

The next ten days were spent at the main campsite that had been booked prior to leaving England. It was called Cococamp a place called Rafina. Set amidst trees and flowers it was quite lovely.

The first night had my bestie's mum frantically hunting for my wristwatch in the dark. It was found lying half-way under one of the van's wheels. I felt sure it would have been smashed to smithereens but luckily it was in one peace. It meant a lot because my mum and dad had bought it for me before I had gone away.

In the days that followed I got to meet some of Cathy's Greek family, and it was on our first visit to her uncle's house that I got to taste red mullet and octopus for the first time after he had treated us to a meal at a' typical' Greek restaurant, as I put it. How could I have said that given that I had never been to one before?

One afternoon Cathy's uncle, aunt and three cousins came to visit us at the campsite and brought with them a dessert that I had never tried before called Baklava. It was delicious.

Her seventeen-year-old cousin Christie made a real impression on me, and I delighted in spending that time playing ping-pong and badminton with him.

The following day we drove through Athens to catch up with the family again, and when we stopped overlooking the Corinth Canal, we found that Christie's aunt had brought with her some souvlaki, which I had never had before – a Greek kebab, I suppose you could say, but not like any I have tasted since. It was delicious.

From there we drove to a park at Epidaurus where Cathy's aunt had prepared yet another meal for us including apple strudel, which we enjoyed shortly before visiting the ancient Roman theatre at Asclepius.

The following day we left camp for Piraeus to catch a ferry. We just managed to make it before the funnel blasted and it set sail. It was indeed a very tiny vessel and the weather was scorching hot. We passed one small island before reaching our destination – Aegina Saint Marina, where we had ice-cream in a small restaurant, as Cathy's folks enjoyed a Turkish coffee.

No sooner had we arrived than we got on a bus, which was more like a coach and took us to the other side of the island. The drive along the cliff-edge road was hair-raising, and on arriving at a restaurant virtually in the middle of nowhere we had a meal of squid, roast beef, chips, bread and salad which was something of a mishmash.

Having had to then do things in reverse, Cathy and I managed to fit in some time swimming and sunbathing on the beach, as we always returned to camp no matter what time of the day or night.

By this time some more of Cathy's family had invited us to their place for dinner and, having gone via Athens again, I was able to catch a glimpse of the Acropolis on top of the hill.

I described their house as being 'like a splendid palace, so big and filled with expensive furniture, carpets and silver ornaments.' We sat on the veranda for a while whilst the grown-ups chatted away indoors and after we were called in for lunch I described 'feeling like a queen sitting on the throne' when I was at the table.

I described the meal as being 'superb' and said I had managed to eat my way through asparagus, ham, salad and cannelloni followed by home-made vanilla and strawberry ice cream which 'the servants brought in soon after clearing the table of the main meal.'

As the grown-ups continued to catch up on conversation again, Cathy's cousin Evie called her and me outside, where she gave my friend a sapphire and ruby ring. I shall never forget it. Then, just as we were about to leave to go back to camp, her aunt took off the ring *she* had been wearing and gave it to me as a 'souvenir to remember her by.' Some souvenir – it was made of pearls.

Cathy's mum told me I could be sure it was 'worth a fortune' if the auntie had been wearing it herself, but I have no idea now what happened to it and I most definitely I did not flog it.

There was a little girl present in the house throughout. I never did figure out exactly who she was, but her name was Mereva, and as we waved 'goodbye' she gave us each a white gardenia that she had picked from the bushes that surrounded the giant house.

We caught up with the first lot of family again just before we boarded the SS *Appia* on the return journey from Patras to Brindisi in Italy, and I shall never forget how warm and welcoming they all were.

I look back on that holiday with fond memories and still harp on about it all these years later. Nothing can ever compare to being eighteen – the excitement of travelling around, of seeing new and wonderful things and experiencing so many different cultures in such a short space of time.

As for my friend and me 'falling in love' with a couple of relative strangers that we had met on the ship, I can see now that it was the environment that provoked such excitement more than anything else. George and Ken, if those were their real names, left us all the time wondering if they could or could not speak English, whether their accents were made up or not, and why one minute they did this and the next minute they did that.

Ken, incidentally, had set his sights on my bestie and I can still picture him in his brown corduroy jacket. We never sailed passed Wuthering Heights and not once did I hear my pal utter the words: 'Heathcliff! I only wish us never to be parted.'

I think if we had come across them in our local 'Golden Egg' enjoying a plate of English fish and chips they would never have looked twice at us, nor us them.

I mean, there was George professing to be one of the sailors on the ship when it turned out he was just one of the cooks and could apparently speak Turkish and Italian but no English, leaving his friend to translate to me that George 'loved me too much' and that it was wrong that I should have to go back to London while he went back to Naples.

I have to say, he asked me for my address before we left the ship and told me he would write first, or at least that is what his interpreter told me. As for Franco, he told me that he would be 'changing to a ship that comes to London' later that year and would come and see me then.

First of all, I had no idea where George really lived and secondly Franco had no idea where my home was, but it didn't stop Cathy and me leaving the *Appia* in tears, heartbroken at the thought that we might never see them ever again. It all sounds quite comical looking back now, but with nothing to compare it to how were we to know it wasn't real' love? But we tried not to let it ruin the rest of our holiday, even though the end was fast approaching.

Once back on dry land, the next campsite we stayed at was in Rimini. We had lunch the following day in Milan, and then spent the following night at a different site in Aosta. We were the only ones camping there that night. The place was set amidst trees and log cabins and 'farmers were constantly tossing hay onto carts', or so I wrote in my diary.

The next night we found ourselves at a campsite just outside Paris. This time we slept in the hammocks that dropped down from the roof in Cathy's dad's motorcaravan, as the weather was atrocious.

Having driven through Arras the following morning we arrived at a place called Béthune, where we stopped for tea before hitching up the 'igloo' style tent at a campsite in L'Escale or Wacquinghen, as my story goes. That was the last place we stayed before arriving back in London on 2nd June 1974 for my then brother Tony's 6th birthday party.

'Dad has painted our living room so beautifully and 'everyone looks so different' I had written, and my diary entry ended with me saying that 'if I could do it all over again I would' and that the £100 that I had given my friend's parents, all-in, had been 'well spent.'

If mum had owned a feather duster back then she could have knocked me down with it, as the saying goes, as surprisingly enough, I *did* get a letter from George asking me to meet him in Southampton.

'So, he loved me after all', I thought, but then my parents forbade me from going and I had to put him out of my mind once and for all. That was the end of that. I do believe Cathy and Ken communicated for a while, but as I recall nothing ever came of it.

CHAPTER 16

WHERE'S MOTHER?

The following year Cathy's folks took me on holiday with them again, this time to Brittany and again by campervan, but with far less 'distraction' than before. Even so the experience was just as enjoyable, as can be validated by my diary entries that I share with you right now.

Monday 4th August 1975

At five minutes to two that afternoon Cathy and her mum and dad picked me up from home, where I was exchanged for her two budgies Billy and Suzie, as my mum and dad were going to look after them while we were on our hols. For the record, I lived in Highgate and Cathy in Edmonton and as for being 'exchanged' for a budgie, well, you know what I mean. The weather was extremely hot as we made our way to Southampton.

Incidentally, I had truly forgotten all about George by this time. He would likely not have turned up there in the first place had I gone against my parents' wishes, and besides, I was now swooning over the boy in the next block of flats – Nick, a couple of years older than me.

The journey was quite straightforward, and at about a quarter to four we stopped at a motorway café along the M3. It was an RAC station and the facilities included a restaurant, a family shop, a take-away meal service and a self-service café.

It was my intention to write the rest of my story verbatim. Whilst I considered my vocabulary to be quite expansive in my late teens, I should hate my readers to think it has not developed 'properly' since then, so I shall hop forward some 45 years and put it in a more 'mature' way.

At the self-service café then, unlike Cathy, who had opted for the apple and blackcurrant tart with cream, the rest of us enjoyed warm pineapple milkshakes and a fruit cocktail jelly. After we had finished eating, Cathy bought an Agatha Christie book to read from the little shop opposite the café while her dad rested for a bit.

At four o'clock we resumed our journey along the motorway, having stopped for tea at a café once we had arrived at Southampton almost three hours later.

The cod and chips left a lot to be desired, the first being almost cremated and the latter severely undercooked, leaving only the taste of the Coke from the tin, as one would have expected.

At seven thirty we arrived at Gate No. 2 at the docks and entered the reception area.

The fact that the place was inundated with French students and school parties meant that there was a delay in us being able to change our money into foreign currency once Thomas Cook had decided to open up their kiosk, somewhat later than we had expected. It did not help matters that Cathy's dad then realised he had parked up in the wrong place for embarkation, which caused some initial panic.

Having found ourselves in the right place, there was an exceptionally long wait to get on the boat, and the crucial moment came as we passed through customs. Cathy's mum had to declare how much English money was in our possession, and since we had more than we should have (not having been able to change as much as we had hoped earlier) she had been a bit reticent with the truth, but she would have been left rather red-faced had she been caught 'fibbing.'

At five minutes to ten we finally boarded the ship and entered the passenger part of it.

I have no idea what Cathy's dad had whispered in the officer's ear after it transpired that Cathy and I were not able to sit together, but whatever it was it worked, and the officer did not turn down the tip that Cathy's dad gave him for sorting it out.

While Cathy's parents went in search of their cabin (number 79), Cathy and I, already having located ours (number 545 for me, number 547 for her) wasted no time in going for a walk around the deck.

The MV *Leopard* was the name of our ship – one of the Normandy Ferries – and I couldn't help being overwhelmed by how big it was. There were five decks in all, A, B, C, D and E, with lifts to take passengers to the upper decks, as one would expect.

As we wandered around the ship we were constantly being followed by a French boy. His age was extremely hard to determine, although I estimated around 17 years old. Wherever Cathy and I went, there he was, and he seemed to find our dashing in and out of doors and up and down steps in a bid to 'escape' him somewhat amusing rather than seeing it for what it was – that he was being a bit of a pest.

It was just after ten thirty when the ship pulled away from the docks and we were on our way to Normandy. The sun had gone in by that time and there were a few drops of rain in the air.

No sooner had we set sail than we met up with another young man, somewhat older than the one above. He had been in the car next to us at the docks. He was also from England and on his way to St. Tropez or some other place 'down south.' I think he was just going where the fancy took him – or even his Morgan sports car!

We made our way to the bar with him in tow to find there was music playing on the juke box, and when the time came that we put our 10p into it after everyone else had had a go. We selected 'Black Pudding Bertha', 'Bye Bye Baby' and 'The Last Day is Coming' to listen to, rather an amusing selection as I read it back now.

After the records had finished at twenty past midnight, we returned to our reclining seats to try to get some sleep, but it didn't help that there was rain pouring down outside and orange streaks of lightning shining through the portholes, nor that the waves of the sea were extremely rough – a rather rocky journey all round and quite scary, if truth be known.

Tuesday 5th August 1975

Despite everything, somehow or other I must have dropped off to sleep, but not for very long. It was partly my own fault I guess, for being cold that night with just my halter-neck top on and nothing covering my shoulders left me with goose-pimples all round, as I had not had the common sense to have taken a cardigan with me. I had thought assuming the foetal position in a limited space would be conducive to a comfortable night's sleep, but this could not have been further from the truth.

My friend, bless her, was also unable to settle and spent much of the early hours wandering up and down the deck looking out for any abandoned blankets for us, but it was not until almost half four in the morning that a man who had evidently been disturbed by our movements and whining went and got a couple of blankets for us from a spare cabin. With that ordeal over and a new day having dawned, a good breakfast was on the cards.

I was somewhat surprised when Cathy's dad had to pay £2.25 to get us into the canteen, before realising that it was to cover the cost of each of our breakfasts at 55p a head. They consisted of little more than a freshly baked croissant, butter, marmalade, a slice of bread and a cup of tea. It doesn't sound a lot today but back in the 70s that was pretty 'steep. Furthermore, unless my maths has let me down, four times 55p is only £2.20, so I wonder what the other 5p was for.

Just saying!

Oh, and who were we to see at breakfast? None other than our cheeky-faced Froggie! This time there was no escaping him.

I forgot to mention that Cathy and I had changed our pocket money, which amounted to all of £15 each, on the boat the day before – 'a quite straightforward operation, I wrote in my diary afterwards.

Operation? I did have a way of exaggerating things, didn't I?

And by the way, £15 was a lot of pocket money back then too.

Breakfast over, Cathy and I went on deck, where I took a photo of the harbour that lay ahead. We got back into the van and disembarked around a quarter to seven, some half an hour later on our way to Caen. Having driven along the motorway for a short period of time we arrived at a toll gate where we had to pay 75p to cross the 1420-metre long Tancarville Bridge – a suspension bridge that crosses the Seine River and connects Tancarville and Marais Vernier in Normandy. The view beneath was breath-taking and not one Cathy and I wanted to miss, having by now fully awoken, after having napped on and off in a bid to catch up on our lack of sleep the night before.

At ten o'clock we stopped in a layby for a drink of pineapple Cresta and some home-made cake. There was a whole field of cabbages to the left of the roadside which looked very out of place! A couple of hours later we arrived at a small village on the way to Sarzeau where we stopped to stretch our legs and buy some food that we later got to eat by a roadside where, as Cathy's dad enjoyed a well-earned rest for a while, Cathy and I got to read some magazines we had bought from home.

Having finally arrived at our campsite in Sarzeau, after Cathy and I had exhausted a game of 'I went to market and I bought...' (you know the one) and bored ourselves by playing the same music cassettes over and over again, we found a nice shady spot to set up the tent, as the sun had been belting down from early morning.

Fortunately, we had found hitching our tent up a lot easier than we had on our previous camping holiday abroad. I cannot believe I actually counted how many pumps it had taken for us to get it erected – six hundred! Between the two of us, Cathy and I must have been extremely fit teenagers!

After our evening meal, which consisted of ham and chips, my friend and I later decided to jump over a wall as several other campers had done as a short-cut to the beach. It was then supposed to be only a five-minute walk away. but we got cold feet and decided to leave it till the morning as it was rather creepy at that time of night. We quickly headed back to camp.

The site was quite small in comparison to others we had stayed up – around 20 square acres I wrote in my diary. It was mainly packed with fellow Brits and French and German holidaymakers.

On returning to camp we discovered a little shop that sold postcards and a place where hot meals were made. There was also a table tennis room which Cathy and I planned on using at some time or another.

A notice had been handed out to the campers telling us that the use of transistors was forbidden after ten o'clock at night, but it had not stopped people from making their own music as we heard in the distance people singing 'Oh my darling Clementine' and 'She'll be coming round the mountain' to a guitar. We listened in our night-dresses.

After that, other than the sound of crickets outside, we had a peaceful night's sleep.

Wednesday 6th August 1975

After waking early as the sun was shining brightly in the sky, once breakfast was over Cathy and I had a very energetic game of badminton before taking a walk to the corner shop, where we bought some postcards and proceeded to write a brief account of events so far to send home to mum and dad. I made a lengthier one in my diary.

As lunchtime came so too did some fellow countrymen to our camp – from Yorkshire to be precise – and they wasted no time in setting their tents up close to ours. I might have enjoyed the lunch that Cathy's mum had prepared – a corned beef salad followed by cake and peaches with evaporated milk – had it not been for a low-flying sparrow which just happened to pass overhead and splat something rather nasty over one of my arms. It was rather off-putting to say the least!

After a further game of badminton, at around half past two my bestie and I decided to go in search of the 'hidden beach' (as I had put it) that we had failed to uncover the night before, although what I guess I had meant to say was one that we had yet to encounter. We finally found it after following a trodden path upon which we found ourselves wading through cornfields with what looked like cabbage patches on either side, or at least that was how I perceived it at the time.

No sooner had we 'sussed' it out than we headed straight back to camp to change into our swimming costumes. We then walked back again, which took us all of fifteen minutes. Why we had not thought to put our cossies on under our clothes and take a towel in the first place I have no idea, but likely because, just as a broader vocabulary comes with maturity, so does common sense.

Despite the sand being an unusual grey colour, it was lovely and soft, and whilst Cathy braved the water I chose to lie lazily on the beach towel until such time as we returned to camp once more, around tea-time. Then we ate, wrote yet more postcards and made further entries in our diaries.

We played yet another game of badminton before the day was out, setting ourselves a target of passing the shuttlecock between us thirty times. We exceeded that it by fifteen, having attracted an audience, which was rather off-putting. When it got too dark for us to see what we were doing we decided to call it a day. We then had a go at making some strawberry milk shakes which we drank before settling down for the night just after ten-thirty.

I have to laugh at the number of insignificant things I wrote in my diary, like Cathy's mum and dad having to resort to cooking for us using Calor gas due to a fault with the gas appliance in their motorhome, and making the mistake of taking a shower on return from the beach, because so intense had been the sun that the water, as a result of solar power, was boiling hot.

Thursday 7th August 1975

The sun was already out by the time we woke at half seven in the morning, and it got hotter as the day progressed.

My account of the day's events was little more exciting than the one before, unless you count Cathy and me going to the local grocer to buy some peaches. Cathy was told off by the woman behind the counter for squeezing them for firmness, as she had seen her folks do many times in the past.

We enjoyed them later in the day after the evening meal of pork chops, potatoes and salad and a small glass of wine as a treat, after which we then drove down to a different campsite on a beach nearby, where we were immediately pounced upon by some French girls who tried to sell us some ice -cream and lollies. We opted for chocolate lollies with ice-cream inside, or so I wrote, which apparently were 'delicious.'

I wrote about us going for a long walk shortly afterwards where we 'ended up almost in the middle of nowhere.' Not sure about the 'almost' bit as you are either in the middle of nowhere or you are not, wouldn't you say, but then you have to remember that my vocabulary was still having teething problems!

I have to laugh, looking back now, how I could have

described it as "like being in the Scottish Highlands" to clamber across rocks and pebbles to get down to the sea's edge, considering I had never been to Scotland in my life – nor have I since.

I feel quite proud of the description I used back then, which painted a picture of an idyllic setting where 'the sun was shining in a white and pink sky, the sea was pale blue and very calm and there were little sailing boats dotted across the water' – all in all a 'very beautiful night' at the beach. I considered it as wonderful as anything one might see on a picture postcard.

Upon returning to our usual campsite, our evening was rounded off with yet another game of badminton.

Friday 8th August 1975

I did not write much on this particular day except to mention a very disappointing trip to Vannes, where we had hoped to have a traditional French breakfast in a little bistro somewhere, only to find that none of them open. The fact that we had arrived there at seven o'clock in the morning likely had something to do with it, given that the French are far more laid back than the Brits and can open and close shops and cafés at their leisure.

For the record, Vannes is a town in Brittany described as 'a magical place where sea, earth and sky mingle in a way that creates a beautiful atmosphere', but we were no sooner in it than out again.

Saturday 9th August 1975

Our travels by this time had taken us first to Port Navalo, where I was really impressed by the sandy gold beach – every inch of it taken up with sunbathers – and yachts dotted across the blue waters as the sun glistened down. I wrote of speedboats, dinghies and lifeboats which had me believe there must have been a sailing club nearby and of a solitary house high upon a hill that I could see in the distance.

On our way from there to Carnac we visited a commune in this north-western part of France called La Trinité, where I mentioned that we stopped in a layby for some cake and a drink, and found ourselves opposite 'some druid monuments.' These were the Carnac stones, built during Neolithic times, which reminded me of Stonehenge, which I had only read about at that time, not imagining for one minute that in time I would be living a stone's throw away from that part of our own national heritage.

In the picturesque Breton town of Dinan we got to meet a Scottish family called the Moodys. They were from Aberdeen, and whilst we had sailed on the *Leopard* from Southampton to France, they had travelled there by Townsend Thoresen. In that short space of time we got to know all there was to know about them and their two kiddies, because Mrs Moody's mouth went into overdrive.

From Dinan we then drove to Caen, once home to

William the Conqueror, where we set up camp once more. From there our holiday trip took us to a little village that had 'hundreds of copper shops', I wrote. I shortened the name of the place to Ville Dieu because I couldn't spell the rest of the name, which was 'les-Poêles.' Well, I guess it was a bit of a mouthful for a nineteen-year-old whose command of the English language was confined to words that did not need 'hats' on top of their letters.

It is unfortunate that my diary has missing pages and so does not cover what we did or where we went in the four days that followed, but by the 14th August we had started our journey back to Southampton, starting at the famous French seaport of Le Havre. Instead of travelling on the M.V. *Leopard* as before, we were instead directed onto the M.V. *Dragon*. Again, Cathy and I were not able to sit side by side but our return seats were fortunately not too far apart.

As we set sail Cathy and I went in search of presents on the ship to take home. I reported 'a long wait at the Spirits and Tobacco counter' but 'managed to buy my dad some rum and tobacco as well as a driving licence and insurance leather wallet' for Nick, my 'boyfriend' at the time. I say 'boyfriend', but he lived in the next block of flats to me and it was more one gigantic crush than anything else.

Having got through customs at Southampton without any problem, on our way back to London we passed through Winchester, where we stopped off at a shop. It was there that I bought my mum a barometer (why?) and sweets for the 'kiddies' (my siblings) – all younger than me.

The red telephone box from which I made a call to my parents before getting back on the road had the usual smell of stale cigarettes, and I clearly remember the panic that set it when a strange woman's voice answered the phone. I remember saying: 'Who is this? Where is my mum? I want to speak to her', and not giving the woman a chance to get a word in edgeways. How mum and I laughed about it over the years that I had not recognised my own mother's voice! I couldn't get home fast enough, fearful that dad had replaced her with some 'floozy' in the short time I had been away. If only common sense had kicked in sooner I should have realised that this would never have happened, as my parents loved each other to the moon and back, and besides it would have taken an even better woman than my mum to have taken on seven children just because of a fling.

My journal ended with me explaining how relieved I was to have finally got home and how, after Cathy had exchanged me for her budgies, I had a bath, washed my hair and was in awe of being back in the comfort of my own home where I did not feel pressurised into having to play badminton. I had always considered it to be, to put it politely, a load of old shuttlecocks!

If I had not gone on those two wonderful holidays with my friend and her folks, I would never have got any further than the courtyard within our little council estate. The positive friendship that Cathy and I had as teenagers certainly played an important role in my journey towards adulthood, and I think it is about time I let her into my secret – that she has featured in more than one of my books, whether intentionally or not, so that she too can reminisce about the good times before it is too late.

I guess it was living on salad, peaches and milk shakes that has left me with a complete dislike for anything healthy like fruit and vegetables and why my palate is more suited to those foods I heard about on the TV like the Txuleton steak – 'home grown' in San Sebastian – or the gastro delights that the Restaurant des Rois on the millionaire's island of Monaco has to offer. I do love red mullet however, and octopus and squid, which I had been able to sample courtesy of Cathy's extended family, so the food I got to eat when I was away was not all bad.

Reading read about all the places that Cathy and I went to and the people we met on our journeys could fool people into thinking we had been on a pilgrimage along El Camino de Santiago.

God forbid!

On a less exciting note it all sounds more like the 'I went to market and bought...' game

Only more a case of 'I went on holiday and met...'

And not unlike: 'As I was going to St Ives...'

You get my drift.

One thing's for sure, not in my wildest dreams would

I ever embark on a pilgrimage and not in a million years will I pick up a badminton racket ever again, although to be fair, I did play a mean 'shuttlecock' in my day.

CHAPTER 17

BLENHEIM

'You can't prevent a bird from landing on your head but you can keep it from building a nest in your hair' and 'if you want to change the world pick up a pen and write' wrote Martin Luther (1483-1546) – two quotes that could not ring more true.

I might as well have been invisible for all the notice anyone has taken of me so far on that road to justice, but there is a danger that if I ruminate much longer my readers might start making excuses for not wanting to come to another of my literary 'pity parties', and that won't do.

Yes, I have been dumped on from a great height, but I have managed to incorporate many more positive thoughts than negative ones into my writing, although I am not quite ready to throw the towel in just yet. If those who wronged my family think they can send me on my way, well they can wash that thought right out of their hair (Rogers and Hammerstein, South Pacific, 1958) and to borrow the phrase made famous by one of our previous Prime Ministers, 'this lady's not for turning.' (Margaret Thatcher, 1980).

So here we are on this 21st day of July 2020 and to catch up, Dame Vera Lynn passed away three days ago at the ripe old age of 103, although she had reportedly been in good health, with no speculation as to whether her death was Covid related or not. The Queen reportedly sent a private message of condolence to the singer's family. Her Majesty had shared her own wartime experiences with the Forces Sweetheart years previously and it was as a result of the bond they had formed that the Queen had no reservations in awarding the singer her title.

Her Majesty's letter of condolence to me on the other hand, as a result of my writing written to her some while after Ted's death, was on a far lesser scale. Whilst she acknowledged my concerns over what had happened to him in hospital, she refrained from offering to help me on the basis of her sovereign status.

"The news of Sir Winston's death caused inexpressible grief to me and my husband. We send our deepest sympathy to you and your family," wrote Her Majesty to Lady Churchill on the death of her husband, and whilst she made no similar mention of 'the whole world being poorer by the loss of my hubby's many-sided genius' because she had never ever met him, everyone knew what a clever chappie he was before and after his 'finest hour' had passed.

At least Sir Winston made it to 90 years and 55 days, whereas Ted did not make it beyond 54, and he would be turning in his grave if he thought for one minute that I had erected a statue in his name, as he couldn't even stand having his picture taken and the only thing that was ever likely to be flying at half-mast would be his trousers if he got dressed in a hurry.

I was only nine when Churchill died, and I can't confess to knowing the ins and outs of his death. His birthplace however – Blenheim Palace – was the first place Ted and I went to when we started courting back in 1976, and it was Ted's love of history in relation to the great leader that attracted us to it in the first place.

The day we went had been the hottest day of an unprecedented heatwave. If only I had remembered to cover the steering wheel of my old Mini 850cc once parked up, we would not have had to spend half an hour on return waiting for it to cool down before I could safely drive us home.

It is strange that I do not remember watching the press coverage of Churchill's death, yet I clearly recall watching the assassination of President John F Kennedy on the telly at a far younger age. I guess the only consolation is that neither Lady Churchill nor I had to witness our hubbies dying at the hands of a sniper. The FBI is no nearer to catching the person who 'really' shot Kennedy any-more than I am at being able to bring to justice the culprits who took my husband away from me at a hospital 70 years on from that incident.

Anyway, back to the here and now.

'Queen for the day' was not a gift bag that I had gone out of my way to buy, but when I saw it while shopping at the local supermarket yesterday I thought it would be rather amusing, if not poignant, to use it as the inner wrap with which to send her Majesty my set of books to date, which I had had every intention of doing from the start, but with the false hope that the last one would have contained a perfect ending. To finish things off I bought a 'thank you' card in which I have now slipped a brief letter I have written to her before wrapping lashings of brown paper and parcel tape around the red glittery box that I have put them into, that which had previously contained a pair of ruby slippers that my eldest daughter had bought me last Christmas. I have even snuck a Marilyn Monroe themed playing card into the front of each book so Her Majesty will know the order to read them in.

Not wanting my gift to fall into the wrong hands, I have been careful to put my address on the back in case for some reason it doesn't reach the Palace and needs returning.

I have tried since early morning to find out where she is staying right now by surfing the internet, but I cannot get a straight answer. I feel sure she is still at Windsor Castle, but I have decided to play safe and send it to the Palace in the hope that she will either have returned or will do one day soon.

Right – all I need to do now is to grab my car keys and get my parcel off in the post.

'Yes, what can I do for you?' asked the gentleman behind the screen at the Post Office, where many a manuscript was sent from before my editor pointed out that it would be easier (and cheaper) for me to email a manuscript in the form of a PDF .

'I want to send this first class signed for please' I said, having handed him what had become quite a large parcel by this time. As he tapped the postcode into his machine for validation, I tried not to laugh when he asked me if I had written it correctly as it had 'not been recognised'.

'SW1A 1AA' I said, confirming it was right as he held it up in front of me. 'There shouldn't be a problem' I said, not expanding on my answer in any way.

It was at that point that he read the address with a distinct Indian lilt in its entirety before exclaiming 'Oh, Buckingham Palace!' I peeped over my shoulder, hoping no one had heard him.

'Exactly 'I said smirking. 'That's why I know the postcode is correct.'

And then, guess what he said. 'It doesn't have any batteries in it, does it?' to which I replied in astonishment, 'No. Just books.'

At that point I was thinking, what on earth did he think I was sending to the Queen – an early toy birthday present for her great-grandson George? Did he really think for one moment that I was about to breach the Dangerous Goods Regulations, given that I had put my address on the back as sender and that it would probably have been intercepted long before it reached her, as royal protocol dictates?

I guess in 'robot fashion' he was just following the set of questions that would ordinarily have been asked, much in the same way that I have been asked at a supermarket check-out if I need a hand with my packing, even though I have only bought one item. This is the world we live in – one that runs on 'tick lists.'

So, having paid the £17.70 postage with the facility of being able to track my package's journey to the Palace, he gently placed it in the Royal Mail hessian sack. There was no going back.

Can anyone else top that for a 'so what did you do today then' story? (smiling emoji).

Another item off my bucket list!

CHAPTER 18

THE SEWING BOX

Does anyone else get sick of reading books about 'the things you need to do before you reach the age of 60?' I certainly hope I get justice for my man before I reach the age of 100 as I am already 63, but that seems as likely as teaching myself to play the guitar before the summer's out, becoming an expert pheasant plucker or being able to break-dance.

There has to be something less ambitious that I can do to fill the rest of my days at home while these stupid social distancing rules continue to leave me so irked, especially as, from tomorrow, I shall have to wear a face covering just to go into my local supermarket.

And they say things are getting back to normal!

Maybe I misheard it on the TV the other day when it was mentioned that cassette tapes are making a comeback, but if that is the case then it will be brilliant as there are some I have kept for almost 40 years, and whilst I have become emotionally attached to the ones that have special significance I was at the point of chucking most of them out, wondering what the point of keeping them was if I was never going to be able to play them again due to all the new-fangled technology. However, it is starting to look as if I can give my sentimental favourites a new lease of life, as it is rumoured that something on the lines of a Sony Walkman might soon be out in the stores by Christmas.

God forbid I should be classed as a 'hoarder' just because I have boxes of cassette tapes in the garage that I haven't listened to since the late 80s, and equally record albums that have not seen the light of day for a lot longer, but there are just some things in life that are eradicable, like memories.

When I look back on my childhood it is the simplest things I remember, like the taste of Farley's rusks, the rhythmic sound of my mum's knitting needles, the smell of roast beef coming from our excuse for a kitchen, the tune from the Tonibell ice-cream van on a Sunday afternoon, the rag 'n' bone man ringing his bell (usually on a Saturday morning), the smell of my brother's cap gun tape, playing hopscotch, jacks, and scissors-paper-stone with my friends and the excitement of going to Woolworths and coming home with baby knitting patterns from which I could produce something stylish for my younger siblings.

I like to think I have a sophisticated and diverse music library, my mum and dad's old 78s included. Unless I can get hold of an old gramophone soon, I shall not be able to play them again either. And what of my Betamax/VHS movie tape collection which was carefully packed away in the garage years ago? It's all DVD players now, so unless I can find someone who can convert them onto a disk they might as well also go in the bin, right now.

Mind you, even if I was able to get hold of the old playback equipment, I doubt my patience would now extend to having to rewind tape through a tiny hole using a wide pen should it start unravelling in the machines, risking me losing my memories altogether.

Talking of tapes, I recall the thrill of taking the kids to the local Blockbuster video rental place when we lived in Plymouth back in the early 90s. There was so much choice, and the option to pre-order something that was not yet out in the cinemas or was 'outdated', like many of the films I myself liked to watch, was perfect.

Stand by Me (1986) and *The Goonies* (1985) were always firm favourites of the kids, as was *Ferris Bueller's Day off* (1986), and we used to make sure we booked the tapes out on a Friday evening since the stores were not open again until the Monday, meaning that the kids got the chance to watch the films over and over again, which they did, before I had to drop them back.

Laura, our eldest, had become a movie fan from a young age and we had a deal going with Blockbusters that once a new film had been hired for a while we could walk away with the large cardboard advertising board in the shop for nothing. Almost 30 years later 'normal' tapes have fallen by the wayside, and my own kids and now grandkids get to watch those films on Netflix from the comfort of their own homes.

Looking back, I wonder whether having allowed my then 12 and 13-year-olds to watch a film that involved a cocky high school undergraduate ringing in sick for the day so he could instead go on a joy ride through the streets of Chicago in a Ferrari he had stolen (with language that left a lot to be desired) was actually appropriate, but there again, every time they eat a Babe Ruth American chocolate bar now memories of their teenage years and that of Chunk and One-eyed Willie continue to bring a smile to their faces.

Perhaps I should bring myself into the 21st century and look at renting the classics in the new-fangled way, but I know the stores won't have any of the films I want (what I really really want, zigazig-ah), because movie value, or so it seems, is no longer measured by the amount of dash, class or sass it contains but instead by the amount of sex and violence involved. All I want is to be able to marvel once more at Bette Davis transforming from a wallflower to a femme fatale, as she has done in so many of her roles.

So, whilst some things are making a comeback, sadly some things are never likely to, such as the Argos catalogue which, after 48 years of being published, will apparently no longer be available in store from now on. Whether it is because more people have taken to ordering things online during lockdown or not I cannot say, but I am just glad that I managed to keep hold of some of them for prosperity.

Just like the Yellow Pages and the Thompson phone directories, the Argos catalogue had become smaller over time, although just as thick, whilst mobile phones seem to be getting bigger day by day.

No one enjoyed flicking through the pages of the Argos catalogues more than hubby and me and the kids at various stages of their growing up. By the time we got married in 1977 I had already filled my 'bottom drawer' with Witney blankets (the ones with the holes in), sheets, pillowcases and a double bedspread (in the days before duvets were invented), which I would pick up from their large store in Holloway in London at a time when I would hop on a bus and drag my siblings around the shops looking for 'wifey' things.

Our first home was largely a replica of his parents' house as they gave us so much stuff to start us off with. We were eternally grateful, as we barely had a penny between us. Even the police house came free of cost. But we both worked hard and saved up for the things we wanted, such as an electric cooker which had one of those eye level grills attached to the top of it – a bit too high to be considered 'eye' level for me though – and a Hoover with a bag that puffed out when pushed.

I always wanted to have one of those Goblin Teasmades, just like my mother-in-law had. She kept it by her bedside and I would gladly have exchanged hers for the set of flying ducks that she had given us to go above our fireplace. I thought it the height of luxury that she could have the first cuppa of the day without having to put her legs out of bed. I on the other hand always got up at the crack of dawn and went downstairs, no matter how cold, to put the kettle on and take a cuppa up to hubby before he went to work so he could enjoy drinking it alongside a fag or two. I wasn't to know at that stage that it was to become a life-long habit – that I had made a rod for my own back, as it were.

I am sure the ironing board and the Morphy Richards iron that mum and dad had bought us for a wedding present came from Argos, as they lasted us for years, so the quality of the stuff was pretty good.

I remember hubby going to the store and bringing me back one of those wooden cantilever sewing boxes just like the one his mum had. I was so happy. I used to love knitting when the kids were small and we both knew she was not going to give hers up lightly any more than her Teas maid, as she kept all her tapestry and crochet stuff in it.

Apart from a brass carriage clock, I don't remember us buying an awful lot from there before the end of the seventies. By the 80s two out of our four children were born and our purchases from Argos then extended to carrycots and circular playpens, high chairs and car seats – not cheap mind – and it was where we bought or eldest, Laura, one of her first Christmas presents – a Jack-in-the-box. At first glance it looked harmless – an innocent toy for an innocent girl – but the way she screamed when the clown popped up after the box was fully wound was pretty loud on the Richter scale. Poor little thing. She was scared half to death.

Taking her on the ghost train at Paignton pier as a three-year old probably wasn't one of our wisest moves either, nor hiring Steven King's 'It' from Blockbusters when she was a teenager. If only her nan on Ted's side had mentioned that the Little Red Riding Hood rag doll she had bought her turned into the big bad wolf when her dress was lifted over her head might have prevented a further traumatic shock.

Hubby was getting into his watches and lighters by that time and decided to treat himself to a Ronson electronic lighter, but he had his eyes more on the Seiko watches that were gloriously displayed in the pages of the catalogue, although they were out of our price bracket.

As the kids got older they started to circle different things that they hoped they would get from us or Santa for Christmas, such as a Petite Typewriter or A-Team and He-Man action figures, while I had my eye on a microwave and a wooden spice rack. We did buy a few bigger items from the store which needed to be delivered, such as our first petrol lawnmower and chest freezer, and it did not take long to feel the pinch of the interest payments after we got ourself an Argos credit card, which took years to pay off.

It seems I was destined to get married and have kids, since stuck on the back pages of my old teenage diaries are pictures of babies in prams and cots and baby dolls (i.e. Tiny Tears) which, believe it or not, I actually remember cutting out of one of the catalogues and sticking in with Le Page glue, so all credit to Argos for that!

CHAPTER 19

CURRY AND LENTILS

Right. So, what else has been on the news in recent days?

At this moment in time, Blackburn and Darwen are now considered to be the top hotspots for Covid-19 after more testing and tracing got underway. Listening to the new updates on TV and of how people from Black, Asian and ethnic minority groups are 'disproportionately' dying from the coronavirus as a result of genetical make-up and associated health risks, perhaps the death toll in such people could have been avoided if only they hadn't eaten so much rice with their curry.

I know this is no laughing matter, but some geek now has us believing that rice contains 'low levels of arsenic', which has been 'linked to 50,000 avoidable deaths worldwide each year from which cancer and cardiovascular disease may have stemmed.

Oh, my giddy aunt! If that is the case could we soon be seeing a name change from Covid-19 to Curry-19 and with a government slogan altered to read:

FORGET RICE – EAT LENTILS – SAVE LIVES

If any of my readers should fall into the BAME category, please try not to panic. I have done a little research of my own. Rice eaten in low quantities also means low toxicity, although a high intake over a number of years does increase the risk of cancer and heart disease as well as Type 2 diabetes, but as the key accompaniment to curry, which has become most popular in Britain more than anywhere else, it could happen to any one of us.

As for the geek's mathematical equation, as I see it, high rice intake = increased levels of arsenic = increased risk of toxicity and therefore decreased intelligence. Perhaps it is something I should put to the Chief Medical Officer when I have a spare five minutes.

Stupid me then, for not having thought about this sooner eh? And there was me thinking I would eventually die from the high cholesterol as found in bacon and belly pork fat, which I love as much as my Basmati.

If curries were hubbies, then I could give Liz Taylor a run for her money. I just cannot get enough of them, even though my taste buds are still in hibernation, and although I am in no way concerned by such 'speculation', I guess there is no harm in me swapping rice for lentils or even cauliflower rice for a while, since it will not affect my current level of enjoyment.

Now that sounds like an intelligent move, wouldn't you say?

I have just heard that Her Majesty has left Windsor Castle, but instead of heading back to the Palace she is instead going to spend the summer at Balmoral as she always does. I read that a handful of her staff will be living there also for the duration – the selected ones who have all been tested for coronavirus and so are 'clean,' but unless her Private Secretary is among them and has taken Her Majesty's post over with her it could be weeks, even months, before I shall learn whether our monarch has opened my parcel or not, let alone read the letter I sent with it.

I know it arrived safely as I was able to track delivery and receipt, as with the fifty-page letter I sent to our Prime Minister at No.10.

I guess all I can do now is to wait and see what happens from here onwards.

CHAPTER 20

CLUELESS

7th August 2020

It's sad I know that on this, the hottest day of the year so far, with the temperature outside in excess of 36 degrees, I should be stuck behind my computer instead of being able to relax in the garden with Ted by my side with a fag in one hand and a pint in the other (me, not him) asking me to fill in the blanks of a daily newspaper crossword.

Ted considered it to be a mark of one's intelligence and capability to be able to do crosswords. He knew full well that I was useless at cryptic clues and used to love gloating as he tried to tell me how he had worked the answers out. Like I really cared!

Sometimes we don't have all the answers we need in life, I know, but I didn't think it too much to ask of the staff at the Firchester hospital, where hubby died, some simple answers to my questions as to what happened after I left him there for the last time instead of explanations of a cryptic nature. Whilst I may not be a genius at solving crossword puzzles in any other context, in this instance the clues were all there, but they were carefully concealed to suit the hospital's own ends. If only I could get someone completely independent to see I am right, it would mean the world to me.

In a newspaper article the other day I read about a Detective Mattson – not a fictional character but a real-life cop – who, like myself, was determined to get to the bottom of a crime no matter how long it took. That is exactly what happened when he managed to recover the missing ruby slippers as worn by Dorothy in The Wizard of Oz that had 'mysteriously' disappeared from The Judy Garland Museum over thirteen years ago.

Now in the hands of the FBI, the investigation continues towards making sure those who were responsible for taking them in the first place are brought to justice.

That same article in the *Daily Express* stated that it was rumoured that the slippers had been stolen to order by the Mafia and even though it might be pure speculation, Di Mattson and two of his faithful colleagues were not frightened into backing off for which I must applaud them.

I have great difficulty understanding where the FBI can go from here, as the newspaper article states 'from a police perspective, the statute of limitations on the original theft has passed, yet this should not prevent them from bringing an extortion case or possession of stolen property charges'. Does this mean that they would also have to fight the judiciary system in the same way as me-then?

My readers will know that The Wizard of Oz is one of my all-time favourite films and in an altered-ego state I *am* Dorothy. The ruby slippers/shoes are made of leather and sequins, not a heart and soul such as those which the staff of the NHS Trust have deprived me of after taking their eye off the ball, so I hope I can be forgiven for being enraged by the fact that an Attorney General can consider it more 'desirable and in the public interest' that valuable tax-payers money should be spent on getting to the bottom of a shoe-hunting exercise than on the death of someone in hospital who has now ended up in that great Emerald City in the sky.

'We will find you, no matter how long it takes or how far you run', and ' We will bring you to justice' – reportedly the FBI's mottos as quoted by the journalist in his article (although not just confined to the matter of Dorothy's slippers). He also mentioned that one of his officers had caught a criminal he had been hunting down for 46 years. He had finally been captured and is now behind bars and facing the consequences of his actions.

Perhaps if I put on my own ruby slippers and click my heels three times that officer will appear in front of my eyes, as he could well be my last hope.

CHAPTER 21

CARRIAGE RETURN

7th August 2020

Perhaps it is coincidence that I have only just written about the typewriter that our eldest got for her 10th Christmas present, or perhaps I was meant to buy that newspaper this morning, because leave aside the ruby slipper article, there is also a full page spread about a 'new' portable adult typewriter. 'No computer required' the advert says, and 'perfectly portable and instantly ready to use.' It goes on to say that 'nothing quite compares to the satisfaction of hearing the soothing click-click sound.' It 'requires no power, is always at hand and complete with all you need to start work straight away.'

The advert goes on to say it is 'perfect for addressing

envelopes, writing letters, making notes or even writing a novel – the list is endless.'

Oh, and it comes complete with a carry case. Semi-equivalent model in the Argos catalogue 1990, albeit with only a 9-inch type bar instead of 11-inch (including carry case), only £49.99. So it seems that whilst tape cassette players are not the only thing set to make a comeback, but should I decide to type future novels up on this new contraption it would set me back £231 (including postage and packaging, mind)!

What makes me giggle is the fact that the inflation rate for the typewriter is equivalent to that of the price I paid for my house in 1998 compared to what it is worth now, the only difference being that my house has been grossly undervalued – this new typewriter is vastly overpriced.

What of the statement that it 'requires no power,' then? What! Not even finger power? Wow!

The machine is 'always at hand', it says. I guess that would depend on whether or not it was kept out on display, as opposed to being stored away between use.

'Complete with all you need to start working straight away,' the ad continues. How can that be when the price doesn't even include any paper? How long will a ribbon last, I wonder? Likely not long enough to tap out a 30,000 (plus) word story such as this, I'm sure, and given there is no backspace and Tippex doesn't come cheap, the length of time it would take to correct any mistakes is unimaginable.

All that before it arrives on the desk of some poor editor, who will then have to edit it by hand with no option of being able to drag and paste the pages in order to create a book 'online' or then upload it for sale on an established website.

I am not one to embrace change easily, but in embarking on a nursing career I was forced to take up computer lessons, which thankfully paid off, else I should not be here today, but considering I can buy a pretty decent laptop for the price of this 'new and exclusive' offer that presents itself in the newspaper, I think I shall give it a miss.

On the other hand, I wouldn't have to worry about a power cut or cyber security, but there again the messy business of having to use carbon paper to create a copy of my work is not a job that I relish going back to.

There again, considering it was a manual typewriter upon which author Frank L Baum wrote *The Wonderful Wizard of Oz*, would it not be criminal to at least give it a go?

CHAPTER 22

THE BIRTHDAY BOY

18th September 2020

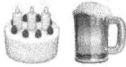

After a few weeks away from the laptop, the first thing I must do today is to wish my hubby a happy birthday.

He would have been 62 years young and ordinarily, as has happened every year since he died, the kids and I would be remembering him with love and affection over a Chinese meal where the waiter waits patiently in the wings for the 'missing' person from the table booking numbers to arrive until we explain why he will not *actually* be turning up, causing embarrassment on both sides. However, with this wretched coronavirus having put the dampers on things this year, and not relishing the thought of having to shove our food down within an allocated time, given the 'eat-all-you-can' menu of over 100 dishes, it leaves me no option really but to dig out the take-away menu and get ordering.

CHAPTER 23

NIGHTMARE ON DOWNING STREET

24th September 2020

As could have been predicted, in recent weeks the wearing of face coverings has become compulsory for shoppers in supermarkets and other indoor spaces, which means I have tried to shop as little as possible. Wearing a mask and glasses is not conducive to seeing, let alone breathing, as the lenses get pretty steamed up and having to take the glasses off, and clean them several times more when the same thing happens does not make the experience of shopping or browsing fun at all.

Schools, universities and gyms have finally opened up and so the grandkids are getting back to some kind of normality, and my own 'kids' are still able to work from home for now, which I am pleased about.

As India and Australia are considered the worst-hit countries at present, in the UK the north-west of England has seen additional restrictions placed upon its communities as the number of coronavirus cases has started to increase. My town, which was on the 'watch list' a month or so ago, is no longer an area of concern, so I guess we are all doing our bit to keep ourselves and others safe.

On a different note, I was indeed happy to see a cream envelope lying on my doormat yesterday bearing the red franking mark of ER. The first thing that caught my eye was the postmark of Windsor Castle on the front of the envelope. Aware that Her Majesty was taking her summer vacation with her hubby in Scotland, I did not have to put on a wax moustache or swap my ruby slippers for a pair of spats and assume a dodgy walk as if I had just had an accident, or fake a French accent to know that she could not be in two places at once, so was a bit confused when the words Balmoral Castle showed up on the letter heading.

'The Queen has asked me to thank you for your letter of *** 2020 from which she had noted your further comments regarding the sad death of your husband and your views on his treatment by the National Health Service'. This was written to me on her majesty's behalf by her correspondent, who as before re-iterated that my case was not a matter the Queen could or would be allowed to become involved in.

Whilst the Queen had considered it thoughtful of me to make her aware of my feelings by sending my books, it would appear from the response letter that the Queen had misconstrued my intentions, as I felt deeply upset to be told that the Queen was 'unable to accept my books as gifts' and that they could not be returned to me as they were considered to be 'unsolicited' items.

All I had done in the letter sent with them was to ask Her Majesty to let me know what she thought of my 'story' – I knew she was not able to act on her 'findings', but more had evidently been read into that letter than I had intended.

Having looked into the whys and wherefores of this, it seems Palace rules dictate that no gifts, including hospitality or services, should be accepted which would, or might appear to, place her under any obligation to the 'donor' or upon which careful consideration must be given to the 'donor', the reason for and occasion of the gift and the nature of the gift itself. Equally, before declining any gift, careful consideration should also be given to any offence that might be caused as a result of any such refusal, yet she really had no reason to be concerned as to my motives for having sent them. I was not after a personal invitation to dinner or a knighthood – just for her to read my story woman-to-woman and to consider how she might feel if the same thing were to happen to her husband when no one wanted to know. That was all!

So saddened was I at having my work not even read, let alone rejected, that I had to make it clear in as dignified a way as I could, so I took the liberty of writing back to Her Majesty's correspondent basically telling her that I had put a lot of effort, sacrifice and expense into getting by books published and that I was giving my permission for anyone in the household to have them rather than for them to end up in the bin. Perhaps that too was overstepping the mark, but it kind of hit me even harder to learn that Her Majesty had willingly accepted a pop-up book from President Xi Jinping to mark the 70th anniversary of communist China back in 2019 and a painting of a swimming pig from the Governor General of the Bahamas, and allowed her hubby to accept an Air Force One jacket from the President of the United States, and yet they want nothing from her in return?

On a different note, still I have had no reply from No.10 about my letter, and whilst the PM has been busy in the past few days liaising with other European leaders in the hope of securing a 'good' business deal before our scheduled exit from the EU on 31st October, I thought someone at least may have replied on his behalf.

I have no doubt there are those who will be horrified if we don't get the deal we need, but there again our involvement has been a bit of a nightmare from start to finish, hasn't it so the fact that this will happen on Halloween is quite timely if not ironic wouldn't you say?

I am not suggesting we got 'tricked' into joining the EU in the first place, but it will be a real treat not to have to hear that word BREXIT ever again!

I would like to be able to say that continually having my concerns over hubby's death dismissed is leaving a bad taste in my mouth, but until I get over this bout of anosmia it would be difficult to verify. After almost five months now with no sense of taste or smell, it is severely impacting on my quality of life, as you can imagine, given that I live for my food as much as I do my kids and grandkids.

I don't know whether it is a sign or not that I should wait a little longer before contacting my GP to consider my 'silent' senses, but having wandered down the 'games' aisle on my way to the DIY section of a local discount store earlier today with the intention of buying a new bulb for my outside light, my eyes were drawn towards a rather small green and black box on the shelf. The actual name of the game I had best not mention yet, due to advertising rights but what I can say is that it is most definitely a party game that should stink for once.

Having spent time so much time online recently researching some of the many 'self-help tips' to help kick start the senses, I am wondering if my latest purchase could be the answer to all my prayers. The sticker on the front was enticing me to remove it and sniff it as a teaser for the other cards included in the game.

I might not have hesitated had my eyes not been drawn at that point towards the WARNING message on the side of the box that says 'delicate noses beware! Player discretion advised.'

As I read in more detail the description on the box, which talked of smells that range from 'nice' to 'downright nasty', I was wondering what kind of fun this can actually bring to the table. The 'stinky stank cards' it speaks of, reserved for those unfortunate few, consists of cards which when scratched, let off odours that can be likened to old cheesy feet, extreme body odour, the unwelcomed 'content' of a baby's nappy and not just any old vomit but the 'heated and lumpy' kind. It mentions a 'timer' but until I open it, I don't know if it is a small egg-timer or what, and with an option to download an 'app' – god knows how that would work.

It's only a game, I know, and I adequately meet the 14+ age criteria, and whilst it is for 2-6 players it is something I would really prefer to tackle on my own, but not until I have had a couple of glasses of metallic-tasting wine first to soften the blow.

Do you know what really puts me off the most? The fact that there is a sticker of the stars and stripes on the side of the box that says the game was compiled partly in the USA and partly in China.

Considering the coronavirus was thought to have started in Wuhan, and given that the US still boasts the highest number of deaths from the deadly disease, I am wondering if my lonely night in will turn out to be a recipe for disaster or whether I have inadvertently stumbled across an antidote that might actually give me hope that one day I shall be back to 'normal.'

Watch this space.

CHAPTER 24

THE NIGHTINGALE RESTAURANT

Thursday 24th September 2020

Was it tempting fate a few weeks ago when the social distancing measures had eased somewhat that I should have turned my garden into what I called The Nightingale Restaurant for just one evening? I utilised my large wooden patio table and my bistro sets to create some atmosphere whilst limiting the 'customers' to myself, my daughter and two 'almost-family' members, as the Nightingale Hospitals are now told to be on 'stand-by' for an expected 'second wave' of the coronavirus.

I felt quite proud of the effort I had gone to try to find some small pocket of happiness for those who, like me, prefer not to eat out at this time. I had great fun sourcing and printing off circular 'Stand two metres apart' and 'Social distancing' stickers online and then spreading them out evenly across the paving slabs.

We sat at our individual tables with a bottle of wine or prosecco on each, and I didn't even have to cook, having ordered a whopping great Chinese takeaway from the place that hubby and I had almost bought shares in over the years. I put on my infection control lead 'hat' as I do at work, and it was paper plates and plastic glasses all the way.

There was music of course, courtesy of Alexa, and photographs did not go amiss as one by one we got to stand in front of my make-shift podium, created using an old CD rack with a Union Jack stuck to the side of it which had not seen the light of day since the Queen's Jubilee celebrations. On the front I had printed the words:

STAY HOME – CONTROL THE VIRUS – DRINK WINE

It was all in good taste and I was trying to send a message that you can still have fun while following the rules with little to no effort whatsoever.

On a serious note, the Prime Minister was not standing behind an old wiry CD rack when just a few days ago he took to putting in what he called a 'raft' of new measures to help tackle the rise in new coronavirus cases which are likely to last for the next six months.

My two eldest had started to go back into the office a couple of days a week, but as of today they are working from home again. From midnight today, all pubs, bars and restaurants are to close by 10pm. The word 'curfew' is now being used, but out of context as in the true sense it means that individuals are required to return to their homes by a certain time and to remain there for a specific period. However, once these venues are shut there is actually nothing preventing those people from visiting others, provided they do not become the seventh person in a group of six, who, at this point in time, do not even have to be from the same household.

The Government slogan has changed yet again over the past few weeks. First it was **STAY HOME – PROTECT THE NHS – SAVE LIVES.** Then: **STAY ALERT – CONTROL THE VIRUS – SAVE LIVES**. Now it is: **HANDS – FACE – SPACE.**

That means washing hands, wearing a face covering, and maintaining adequate social distance.

Finally, those working in the hospitality and retail sector must now wear face coverings too and not just shoppers, which ensures double protection against the virus. I am so glad, as this will stop certain staff members from using discriminatory practice by asking a select few, as I have witnessed, to remove their masks briefly so that their faces can be seen, as if they are about to rob the place.

If I were brave enough, and just for the sake of argument, I would so love to be able to ask those 'certain' members of staff to now remove *their* masks for a bit so that customers can see *exactly* who is *serving* them!

On the subject of anti-social behaviour, we won't have to worry about the prospect of football hooliganism for the time being now that Mr J has put the kibosh on many of the top clubs welcoming fans back to the stadiums, as was supposed to happen on 1st October, although the number of spectators would have been restricted to 1,000 – but now no longer.

I hope my brother and sisters can get some money back for wasted season tickets for Chelsea F.C., as there is a suggestion that the ban could run well into 2021.

Mr J is reported to be 'broken-hearted' at having had to restrict family gatherings at this time, and as I have barely got over writing about Christmas 2019 in 'Pennies From Heaven' (Book 6), the prospect of being able to enjoy the forthcoming event – just over three months away - in the same way seems pretty unlikely.

Unless by some miracle, the virus leaves people alone not just on 39th Street in New York but across all the streets in the UK, Santa's wife had better prepare to knock up some red and white face-coverings for herself, Santa and his little helpers, as well as ones that can comfortably be worn over reindeer antlers.

At the risk of another full lockdown I had better get my skates on then and stock up on what I need to make my Christmas cakes, sausage rolls and mince pies. I will definitely need enough Snowballs and Babychams to see me through the hard times even if I might still not be able to distinguish one from the other by that time. I am keeping everything crossed that I will.

CHAPTER 25

KEEPING TRACK

Friday 25th September 2020

Amidst privacy concerns, the Track and Trace 'app' that the Government had hoped would be up and running in the UK back in June was finally launched yesterday. It is in essence just what is says – a tracking system that alerts users to the fact that they have come into contact with someone who has had a positive Covid-19 test result or have signed into any venue that is considered to be a coronavirus 'hotspot'. In this case they will be asked to self-isolate for two weeks.

It talks about 'digital handshakes' sent via Bluetooth if you come into contact with another app user for more than five minutes, and it can apparently work out exactly how close to one another you were, as well as how many times and for how long you have interacted with other people over the course of 24 hours.

The Government has probably spent millions trying to get it up and running, but I fail to see how it will work, especially since downloading the app is voluntary, not mandatory. Just like GPS on a mobile phone, I see it as a clever way to keep tabs on people to make sure that they are not breaking the 'gathering' rules first and foremost, but I could be wrong.

If the app is designed to monitor and ensure a person's safety, and if I were the Health Secretary, I would compel all NHS hospital staff to download it, if only because when there is conflicting information as to what wards a patient did or did not visit, especially if it has resulted in a cardiac arrest from which they died, the digital evidence is there.

If only that had been possible back in 2012, I might not still be sitting here today trying to argue the point within a complaint system that hubby could not possibly have arrested on a ward he never went to nor be discharged from a further one he never visited, which heavily conflicts with the written timeline of his movements within the NHS Trust.

There should be a board on the wall outside every ward with a QR code on it that staff will need to scan on their phones each time they go back and forth through the doors to prevent future discrepancies.

Hey, perhaps I should write to Mr H right now and see what he thinks. There again, logical reasoning is not really his strong point as was he not the one who told the press when asked about the importance of hand-washing that the impact of getting Covid-19 from shaking hands was 'negligible', suggesting that as long as hands were washed more often it was still acceptable.

CHAPTER 26

BEAM ME UP, SNOTTY

Star date: 280920

Ok, so perhaps I haven't fully grasped the whole Star Trek thing and there may be one digit too many, but I am sure even the non-'Trekkie' fans among you can figure out what day it is today without me having to spell it out.

'Beam me up snotty' was my hubby's take on Captain James T Kirk's catchphrase as used in the television series at times when he wanted his Chief Engineer, Mr Scott, to transport him and his Vulcan colleague Mr Spock back to the Starship Enterprise after they had completed any one of their many missions on various alien planets to rid them of wrongdoers/baddies.

I myself have also been trying to put the world to rights, in the interests of the general public, to try and find a cure for clinical incompetence and judiciary ignorance through the wonder of the pen, but to little avail. So whilst I remain frustrated here on Planet Earth I have seized the opportunity earlier to pour myself some raspberry gin that was lurking at the bottom of the bottle and then opened the box on the 'stinky game' that I had previously put aside with some trepidation.

Having spent a good half hour or so afterwards sniffing the cards one by one which released a different scent when scratched with a coin, whilst I was not always able to put my finger on exactly what it related to, I was able to determine at least that things were either chemical, spicy or just 'plain stinky' as far as categories went.

In the DETERGENT category my mind conjured up the smell of Ajax (other abrasive cleaners are available), although the answer on the card was not that specific.

I got the smell of coconut on another card straight away, and with eyes closed at the time of sniffing I did feel as if I was lying on a sun-kissed beach instead of being sat on a rock-hard chair.

I hesitated at the next smell, finally opting for the fragrance of lavender, but after seeing baby powder on the answer list, I thought it reminded me of Johnson's (other brands are also available), so that was pleasing.

In the SPICE IT UP category I did pretty well too. After getting a whiff of something that seemed familiar, I immediately thought 'that's curry', and given the answer was cumin, that was reassuring.

I have always hated the smell of cloves and cinnamon, so I did not let myself down too badly in that section nor in the SMOKE FACTOR category when the smell of something barbecuey/smoked came to mind – something I also detest, and the smell of hot dogs especially. The category that I did fail miserably in though was the SWEET STUFF. I was not able to pick up the scent of bubble gum, strawberry, fruit juice or Tutti-Frutti (even though I used to love the taste of Rowntree's Tootie Frooties as a kid), and despite having used marzipan on so many occasions when icing my Christmas cakes over the years, I could detect neither the smell of almond paste nor amaretto.

What I did come up trumps in though was the category entitled JUST PLAIN STINKY, which covered 'dirty socks', 'body odour' and 'flatulence' – the latter a familiar smell that I associated with our late Border Collie Bert after he had eaten one too many marrow bones.

I would much have preferred to have been able to pass the test in the BLOOMIN' FRESH section, but not only did the smell of flowers and lemon escape my nostrils, but also the scent of freshly cut grass, which I should have been more than familiar with after years or having been the one who took responsibility for cutting the lawn wherever Ted and I ended up living.

Sitting at the dining table with reading glasses on ready to write my answers instead of wearing a white laboratory coat, I was playing the game in my black and white fluffy pyjamas but nevertheless I felt rather like Jerry Lewis in the original version of *The Nutty Professor* as I carried out my experiment In the 1963 film, the Professor had decided to create a serum which, when drunk, would turn him from an accident prone 'geek' into someone handsome, charming and suave, but much as I would prefer to be far better looking, more sophisticated and desirable, the goal of my own experiment was simply to put my sense of smell to the test.

Just as my editor will have the final say in determining whether or not I have structured my book properly and whether what I have written has been broken down into the right chapters, I shall wait until I have sniffed the entire contents of the game before presenting my experimental report to the world. I am not sure that I will be able to present my results in such an effective and coherent way as the scientific advisers in charge of updating us on how the Test 'n' Trace system is working, but one thing's for sure when it comes to documenting how I performed it, the results I obtained and their importance in relation to why I had done this in the first place, one thing's for sure it will have a style all of its very own.

Scientific writing is a whole new ball game for me, difficult to grasp, since I am already mixing up IMRAD as a research acronym with IMROD which is a giant unrepentant creature who wields a giant hammer as flames shoot from his helmet as features in–the Play Station 4 game *Mortal Shell*.

As for 'inverted pyramids', the only pyramid I am familiar with is the one that addresses Maslow's Hierarchy of Needs.

What if the rest of the cards that I have yet to sniff reveal more than I bargained for and what if somehow or other the light-bulb in my nostrils should suddenly be re-ignited as a result of this game and my experiment? Might I then be able to go on and patent it in a different way for the good of those like me who have been cheated of their basic senses as a result of Covid-19?-

Who knows, but to echo the words of Del Boy Trotter (*Only Fools and Horses, TV series*) – 'this time next year I could be a millionaire!

CHAPTER 27

IN LOVING MEMORY

My writing has taken me on a journey which at times has been devastating, but in drawing inspiration from everyday things around me – none more so than at a time like this – it has also been uplifting, because if nothing else I have had the opportunity to include funny snippets of information that can go down in history.

Considering all the misery that is going on in the world at present and all the people who are clutching at straws to get a job during this new kind of economic decline, I felt sorry for the owner of a hair salon who was recently slated for advertising for a new stylist who must be of a 'happy' disposition. She was forced to remove the ad on the basis that it was discriminatory against those who are miserable.

It reminded me of something I had read when I was younger. Under the Sex Discrimination Act 1975, bosses were no longer able to get away with specifying in their ads that they were looking for 'pretty' secretaries, but they were able to get around it by asking instead for candidates to 'include a recent photograph with your application.' Same difference eh?

But there again anyone can fake a smile, whereas the camera cannot lie.

Considering all the rules that are being flouted right now during this time of 'corona' their acts seem quite trivial by comparison. Yet it seems it is still acceptable for bosses of NHS Trusts to flout the rules when it comes to reporting patient safety related hospital deaths. Those left behind are discriminated against in seeking justice for their losses simply because they cannot afford to take such a powerful body to court, and there is absolutely no way round that one, especially where excessive secrecy inhibits information sharing with those who might be able to contribute to the successful conclusion of a case.

The thing is, if the staff hold their **HANDS** up to what they have done they know they will have to **FACE** the consequences, and whilst I am sure they would love to be able to send me on a journey into some new dimension, like outer **SPACE** – I am not going anywhere!

Furthermore, if I can remember so clearly what happened on my holidays back in the 1970s then I defy them to question any dates, times or places that I can put my finger on to support exactly what had happened to hubby in respect of the wheres, whens and whos.

Wednesday 30th September 2020

The last few days have seen the Prime Minister look rather embarrassed, having been criticised for not fully understanding his own social distancing rules as imposed on those living in the north-east of England.

Hundreds of University students are now in lockdown due to positive cases of the virus on campus; pubs and restaurants have been ordered to close at 10pm (although it has not stopped people from spilling out onto the streets afterwards to continue their partying), and there is a good chance we will be seeing more of Mr J and his expert advisers giving parliamentary updates on the 'R' rate, just as we did back in March, now that things are heading in the wrong direction.

I have a sneaky feeling the state of the nation is about to get a whole lot worse before it gets better, but hey ho. Just need to go with the flow!

It would just be nice to get back to some normality in which women are driving their commuter husbands to stations and their children to school, where they can then have a natter with other mums without having to talk through linen. It would be nice for vans to be delivering something other than Covid-19 testing kits and no end of online shopping from Amazon. It would be nice for buses and coaches to be able to load and discharge passengers before or after a good night out where friends have all been able to sit together instead of miles apart, and to be able to feel safe in a cab without having to wonder who is behind the mask.

As for me, the pleasures I seek in life are quite simple really, like watching the soaps on TV. It looks like Cain and Moira could get back together after all, which is great, although I am saddened to see that DI Malone is now six foot under in Harriet's own churchyard cemetery after the ex-detective vicar hit him over the head with a heavy object and her partner Will's daughter shot him three times because he tried to get her high on drugs.

At least they had the common sense to wrap him up in a thick piece of carpet before offering him up as worm feed, so there is no chance of him getting frostbitten now that winter is setting in in the village of Emmerdale.

I am pleased to see that Sharon has got her pub back in Eastenders, as the previous owner, 'L', was seriously getting on my nerves, and just so as you know, the actor who plays the nasty Ian Beale is nothing at all like his TV character in real life – my youngest can vouch for that because she got to serve him in her café the last time he played the wicked queen's henchman in a Christmas pantomime at our local theatre.

I have no doubt that the handsome Seik Kheerat will see that the smarmy and abusive lawyer Gray pays dearly for leaving his wife to die after learning of their almost non-existent love affair, and it would be great if Masood were to return to the square and open up the 'Argy Bargy', his Indian restaurant, again, even if the regulars of Albert Square would have to leave at 10pm with a doggy bag.

As for 'Corrie', I am living for the day when Jiggle-it Geoff fails to jiggle any keys outside his prison cell. He should be made to face the consequences for what he did to his wife Yasmeen, who needs to get back to Speed Daal as the 'eat-out-to-help-out' scheme that does *not* form part of the script continues to run for a while longer in Kerry-land.

She could do well to hire the gorgeous Mancs from Mumbai as waiters now that they have had a chance to explore their Indian heritage for real, and it is not as if Eileen wouldn't welcome her son Jason back with open arms, while younger son Todd is still nowhere to be found.

As for his real life brothers, Adam might stand to get paid a lot more if he were to leave Emmerdale for Corrie and as for Scott, I shouldn't be at all surprised if Love Island is next on the local lockdown list, given how close everyone gets to each other, else the girls will have to start wearing their bikini bottoms as face masks which, let's face it, would still be too small.

Alia would get to take her pick of the guys whilst I look on jealously, but I feel confident that the ratings would go up even more. You could say, a case of winner, winner, chicken Madras dinner.

Talking of which, I might then get a chance to send the boys my chicken vindaloo recipe, which they could cook and test and convince Yasmeen to stick on her menu board.

Oh well, perhaps things like this can only happen in the world according to Doreen, but it doesn't hurt to dream now, does it?

At this precise moment in time I am forcing my eyelids open and resisting the urge to go up the wooden hill and wiggle down into the enveloping warmth of my bed to let my mind drift into blessed unconsciousness before morning comes, when I must once more force myself to put on a generous dollop of foundation, a small amount of concealer and a sensible amount of blusher and lippy to face another day wishing it could be to the smell of burnt toast which under any other circumstances I absolutely loathe.

I shall pray tonight, as I have for so many nights, that I might also wake up and get a whiff of cigarettes coming up from downstairs as hubby sits at the dining table having one last fag before finishing his cup of tea and heading off to work. The only thing I have had a good nose for over the past years has been the smell of injury and a strong odour of injustice. If only I could bottle it and sell my story to the highest bidder I might eventually get to sleep at night.-

Talking of bottling things, I have to laugh (although I shouldn't really), as the worldwide news reports that the President of the United States has returned to the White House after a spell in hospital to continue his recovery from himself, having received a positive

Covid-19 result a few days ago. As he had received a drug called Remdesivir (as used to treat the Ebola virus some years ago) as well as an 'experimental' cocktail for which neither bleach nor disinfectant would have been added, I bet he was bottling it, wondering if he would be fit enough to resume his campaign in is fight to be elected for a second time or whether his rival Mr Biden might pip him to the post. There is speculation, of course, as to whether or not Mr T had even got Covid-19 or not or whether he was just banking on the sympathy vote from his supporters in order to secure a second term in office which just begs us to answer the question as to whether or not it was he this time who had created some 'fake news' all of his very own!

I guess only time will tell.

11th October 2020

Talking of time – as the kids and I remember this, the 8th anniversary of Ted's death, in some ways it seems like only yesterday, as sitting around his bed waiting for the nurses to turn his machine off still seems raw.

In a year like no other, our plan later is to get together at the place he called 'home' where we won't have to worry about getting taxis to and from that same favourite Chinese restaurant that we might otherwise have gone to, just as he would have on his most recent birthday, or have to worry about registering a QR code on the way to the dining table.

My plan for today then is to spend the day cooking some of his favourite dishes from the well-fingered pages of the Chinese cookbook – dog-eared over the years – and do him proud as we gather together, thankful that the virus has managed to bypass all but me for now. There will be music playing in the background – Billy Fury, Elvis, Del Shannon and Buddy Holly – just some of his favourite singers for which the kids and I know every word to every song even if he didn't always.

As his jacket remains on the back of the dining chair at the head of the table where he used to sit we will also lay a place for him – to the rest of the world, the Unknown Warrior who lost his fight for life amidst clinical incompetence – and put a 'reserved' sign of the place mat as we usually do alongside a bottle of beer and an empty glass.

7th November 2020

The welcomed advantage of an author over a journalist is that there is no pressure to get a story out to the press and during the course of heavily revising what I presented to my editor a few weeks ago, I have taken on board his comments on some of the style and usage that he came across whilst respecting my personal style of writing. I respectfully ask that he forgive me for extending the timeline of my story in the process of heavily revising it so it makes more sense.

In having sneakily done so, I have been able to validate first-hand that history does indeed repeat itself, since 8 months on, when it was hoped that the word coronavirus would be a thing of the past, the Prime Minister has been forced into announcing a second lockdown in England. In his speech he acknowledged how 'tough' it would be and how anxious, weary and 'quite frankly fed up' at the mention of the virus everyone was, whilst offering hope that the measures would be less stringent and that the country should be optimistic that if people followed the rules properly, the lockdown should be lifted in time for 'families to get together at Christmas' if not before.

Well, the lockdown has put the dampers on things already as far as I am concerned.

If it wasn't enough that the youngest of my grandkids couldn't go trick or treating this year due to the rules on social distancing, granddaughter Lola has had to forgo a proper birthday party with even the smallest number of friends.

As for my youngest 'child', her 35th birthday on 11th November will be a day she will not be able to remember as one shared with good friends over a decent bottle of prosecco or two, and plans for grandson Jay's 18th birthday celebrations at the end of the month have had to be postponed.

They say everything happens for a reason – but the reason has been that so many people have not taken seriously how deadly and sneaky the virus is and carried on living their lives as 'normal', so the rest of us are now continuing to pay the penalty for that.

So in rounding up the news at it stands at present, the previously 'eat out to help out' scheme that had encouraged people to support their local restaurants by dining with them despite safety measures in place has since become a matter of 'eat out and get out' as restaurateurs have been forced to close their doors again.

Once more Mr J has also called 'last orders' on pubs being able to operate and non-essential shops being allowed to open. and he has enforced no household mixing unless for child-care and still not exceeding the rule of six. Yet, the schools, universities and colleges are allowed to remain open, so getting the 'R' rate down will work – how?

So little has changed in the past seven months. If the coronavirus were a person it would have been shot by now for all the harm it has caused and for the interruption to our daily lives.

I still have to go to work whilst others are now back in the privileged position of being able to work from home as the furlough scheme has been extended to March 2021; the self-employed are in a better position than before as their entitlement to income support has gone up from 40% to 80% of their normal wage; my youngest is still not entitled to a penny since her business has not been running for long enough despite her clients cancelling on her yet again; there will be no free school meal vouchers, since the schools will provide students with their meals from now on whilst young 'Rashford' who had campaigned for them first time around has walked away with an MBE; I am no nearer to getting Justice for the loss of my husband and my sense of taste and smell is still zilch after almost seven months!

On the celebrity front my favourite James Bond – Sean Connery (or should I say Sir Sean) died in his sleep at the age of 90 this Halloween, the day Britain finally left the EU. Footballer Nobby Stiles, who played in the 1966 World Cup final, passed away the day before at the age of 78 from cancer but had also been diagnosed with dementia. Legendary TV presenter Frank Bough died on 21st October at the age of 78. Hollywood legend Rhonda Fleming died the week before at the age of 97. "I can see clearly now" singer Johnny Nash reached the age of 80 before dying on 6th October. Sir Bobby Charlton (considered to be England's greatest ever footballer) is now living with dementia, and comedian Bobby Ball of Cannon and Ball fame became the latest victim of the coronavirus at the age of 76, and sadly never recovered.

Each one will go down in history as having died during the pandemic – sad at the best of times, as these were the very people who I had grown up with in a roundabout way.

However, on a brighter note, whilst the reason for the delay in my daughter being able to pick up the keys for the purchase of her first home a few weeks ago is not known, it was quite poignant that it just so happened to be on the 22nd October 2020. Not only was it the day of Ted's funeral but also what would have been our 43rd wedding anniversary, so her dad was definitely looking down on her that day, as I know he is on the rest of us, making good things happen when we need him the most.

STAY HOME – PROTECT THE NHS – SAVE LIVES

The government slogan from the first lockdown in March is now being recycled, but I won't let it dampen my spirits. I will finish this volume of my series on the humorous note that I had intended, had I not decided to extend things. It is to clap your **HANDS** if I have managed to put a smile on your **FACE** without boring you to death, and if you would like to read what happens next, just watch this **SPACE.**

Arrivederci!

www.ingramcontent.com/pod-product-compliance
Lightning Source LLC
Chambersburg PA
CBHW061432040426
42450CB00007B/1017